The Seventh 200 Questions Answered By Dr. D. A. Waite

?

Real Questions From Real People With Real Answers

Published by

THE BIBLE FOR TODAY PRESS
900 Park Avenue
Collingswood, New Jersey 08108
U.S.A.
Pastor D. A. Waite, Th.D., Ph.D.
Bible For Today Baptist Church
Church Phone: 856-854-4747
BFT Phone: 856-854-4452
Orders: 1-800-John 10:9
e-mail: BFT@BibleForToday.org
Website: www.BibleForToday.org
FAX: 856-854-2464

We Use and Defend
The King James Bible

October, 2016
BFT 4151

ISBN #978-1-56848-110-4

Acknowledgments

I wish to acknowledge the assistance of the following people:

• **Yvonne Sanborn Waite**--my wife, for encouraging me to publish these questions and answers, for reading the manuscript carefully; and for giving other helpful suggestions for the body and the cover of this book.

• **Bonlyn Walls**—one of those who attend our church services via the Internet. She has been a great help in proofreading some of Pastor Waite's verse-by-verse Bible books. We are grateful that she has now volunteered to help in proofreading this *Seventh 200 Questions Answered Book #7* as well.

• **Dr. Kirk DiVietro**—a friend for many years, one of our Dean Burgon Society Vice Presidents, who is an expert on the use of computers. He has helped in various ways to make the computer work easier when performing the needed tasks.

FOREWORD

• **Eleven Sections.** I have divided the questions up into eleven general topics. This is the seventh series of 200 questions that have been sent to me (## 1201-1400). I have answered them as simply and as clearly as possible. For ordering the other six *200 Question and Answer Books*, click the LINK below and scroll to find the titles. http://biblefortoday.org/idx_Pages/idx_featured_boo ks.htm

• **The Order Of Questions.**   Based on the importance of the question topics, I have listed question topics in this order: (1) Salvation, (2) the Lord Jesus Christ, (3) the King James Bible, (4) the Hebrew and Greek Texts, (5) Other Bible Versions, (6) Other Doctrinal Positions, (7) Local Church Decisions, (8) Various Moral Questions, (9) Questions About Meaning Of Terms, (10) Questions About The Constitution, and (11) Miscellaneous Questions.

• **Various Questions and Answers Are Similar.** I have tried not to duplicate questions and answers in this seventh *200 Question And Answer Book*. However, various things should be understood by the readers–similar questions might have been asked in books one through six; similar questions might also have been asked in this seventh book. But if there is a slightly different emphasis either in the question, or in my answer, I have included them.

• **Consult The Detailed Index For Topics.** Be sure to consult the very detailed Index (p. 155) in this book to help you find where various subjects are located.

Pastor D. A. Waite, Th.D., Ph.D.

Director of the Bible For Today, Incorporated, and Pastor of the Bible For Today Baptist Church

Table of Contents

The Seventh 200 Questions Answered By Dr. D. A. Waite

?

Introductory Considerations

This question and answer book is the seventh in a series. Each of the previous books had 200 questions and 200 answers about a variety of subjects and themes. Every one of these 1400 questions and many others, have been asked of me throughout the past years. In case you want to know how to receive copies of the first seven of these question and answer books, here is how you can order them.

1. *THE FIRST 200 QUESTIONS ANSWERED* book is **(BFT #3909 @ $15.00 + $7.00 S&H),** (questions #1-200).

2. *THE SECOND 200 QUESTIONS ANSWERED* book is **(BFT #3473 @ $15.00 + $7.00 S&H),** (questions #201-400).

3. *THE THIRD 200 QUESTIONS ANSWERED* book is **(BFT #3482 @ $15.00 + $7.00 S&H),** (questions #401-600).

4. *THE FOURTH 200 QUESTIONS ANSWERED* book is **(BFT #3494 @ $15.00 + $7.00 S&H),** (questions #601-800).

5.   *THE FIFTH 200 QUESTIONS ANSWERED* book is **(BFT #4104 @ $15.00 + $7.00 S&H),** (questions #801-1,000).

6.   *THE SIXTH 200 QUESTIONS ANSWERED* book is **(BFT #4058 @ $15.00 + $7.00 S&H),** (questions #1001-1200).

7.   *THE SEVENTH 200 QUESTIONS ANSWERED* book is **(BFT #4151 @ $15.00 + $7.00 S&H),** (questions #1201-1400).

To order any of these question and answer books, you can:

(1)   Phone in your order at **856-854-4452**.

(2)   Mail your order to Bible For Today, 900 Park Avenue, Collingswood, New Jersey 08108.

(3)   FAX your order at **856-854-2464**.

(4)   Go directly to the Bible For Today Webstore at http://biblefortoday.org/search.asp and order by Internet.

CHAPTER I
QUESTIONS ABOUT
SALVATION

God's Salvation's Vital Principles
QUESTION #1201

I am from Kenya, Africa. I need to cross over to Jesus now. Kindly help me to receive Christ. Help me fully to understand it properly. Our family is Muslim. I knew Mohammed as my god. It is my first day to see Christ. In a short while, I'll share my faith with my wife. She became worried after I fell down on my knees praying. She thought I was sick.

ANSWER #1201

Here are a few very important beginning things to understand about receiving eternal life by genuine faith in the Lord Jesus Christ as your Saviour:

1. You must realize that God considers you, and all the people of the world, to be sinners who cannot save themselves. If they are not saved, they will go to the everlasting fires of Hell.

2. You must realize that the Lord Jesus Christ died on the cross and carried your sins and the sins of the world in Himself, paying the penalty for your sins and the sins of the whole world.

3. After you have genuinely believed these first two things, you must, from your heart, genuinely accept, believe on, and trust the Lord Jesus Christ as your Saviour. He died in your place on the cross so that you would not have to pay for your sins in everlasting Hell fire.

Here are 32 verses about salvation that you can read, study, and genuinely believe. I hope you can lead your wife to become a genuine Christian as well by the understanding and use of these verses.

1. **John 3:16** *"For God so loved the world, that he gave his only begotten Son, that whosoever believeth in him should not perish, but have everlasting life."*

2. **John 3:17** *"For God sent not his Son into the world to condemn the world; but that the world through him might be saved."*

3. **John 3:18** *"He that believeth on him is not condemned: but he that believeth not is condemned already, because he hath not believed in the name of the only begotten Son of God."*

4. **John 5:24** *"Verily, verily, I say unto you, He that heareth my word, and believeth on him that sent me, hath everlasting life, and shall not come into condemnation; but is passed from death unto life.*

5. **John 10:27** *"My sheep hear my voice, and I know them, and they follow me:"*

6. **John 10:28** *"And I give unto them eternal life; and they shall never perish, neither shall any man pluck them out of my hand."*

7. **John 10:29** *"My Father, which gave them me, is greater than all; and no man is able to pluck them out of my Father's hand."*

8. **John 10:30** *"I and my Father are one."*

9. **John 14:1** *"Let not your heart be troubled: ye believe in God, believe also in me."*

10. **John 14:2** *"In my Father's house are many mansions: if it were not so, I would have told you. I go to prepare a place for you."*

11. **John 14:3** *"And if I go and prepare a place for you, I will come again, and receive you unto myself; that where I am, there ye may be also."*

12. **John 20:30** *"And many other signs truly did Jesus in the presence of his disciples, which are not written in this book:"*

13. **John 20:31** *"But these are written, that ye might believe that Jesus is the Christ, the Son of God; and that believing ye might have life through his name."*

14. **Acts 4:12** *"Neither is there salvation in any other: for there is none other name under heaven given among men, whereby we must be saved."*

15. **Acts 13:39** *"And by him all that believe are justified from all things, from which ye could not be justified by the law of Moses."*

16. **Acts 16:30** *"And brought them out, and said, Sirs, what must I do to be saved?"*

17. **Acts 16:31** *"And they said, Believe on the Lord Jesus Christ, and thou shalt be saved, and thy house."*

18. **Acts 16:32** *"And they spake unto him the word of the Lord, and to all that were in his house."*

19. **Romans 3:22** *"Even the righteousness of God which is by faith of Jesus Christ unto all and upon all them that believe: for there is no difference:"*

20. **Romans 3:23** *"For all have sinned, and come short of the glory of God;"*

21. **Romans 3:24** *"Being justified freely by his grace through the redemption that is in Christ Jesus:"*

22. **Romans 3:25** *"Whom God hath set forth to be a propitiation through faith in his blood, to declare his righteousness for the remission of sins that are past, through the forbearance of God;"*

23. **Romans 3:26** *"To declare, I say, at this time his righteousness: that he might be just, and the justifier of him which believeth in Jesus."*

24. **Romans 6:23** *"For the wages of sin is death; but the gift of God is eternal life through Jesus Christ our Lord."*

25. **1 Corinthians 1:18** *"For the preaching of the cross is to them that perish foolishness; but unto us which are saved it is the power of God."*

26. **Ephesians 2:8** *"For by grace are ye saved through faith; and that not of yourselves: it is the gift of God:"*

27. **Ephesians 2:9** *"Not of works, lest any man should boast."*

28. **Ephesians 2:10** *"For we are his workmanship, created in Christ Jesus unto good works, which God hath before ordained that we should walk in them."*

29. **Galatians 3:26** *"For ye are all the children of God by faith in Christ Jesus."*

30. **1 Timothy 1:15** *"This is a faithful saying, and worthy of all acceptation, that Christ Jesus came into the world to save sinners; of whom I am chief."*

31. **Luke 19:10** *"For the Son of man is come to seek and to save that which was lost."*

32. **1 Peter 2:24** *"Who his own self bare our sins in his own body on the tree, that we, being dead to sins, should live unto righteousness: by whose stripes ye were healed."*

Here are 32 verses about salvation that you can read, study, and genuinely believe for God's promise of salvation to the one who genuinely believes on, trusts, and accepts His Son, the Lord Jesus Christ as Saviour. I hope you can lead your wife to become a genuine Christian as well.

Leading The Elderly To Christ
QUESTION #1202

I have a question about a rest home ministry. I am starting to play harmonica and sing. I want to find a way to tell the elderly about salvation. I need some help and guidance. Do you have any thoughts?   **ANSWER #1202**

If you want to tell the elderly about salvation, I suggest that you begin with the Gospel of John. You can use key verses about salvation like John 1:1-14, John 3:1-18, and John 5:36. There are many other salvation verses in this Gospel. I think Bible study with the elderly, using verses will enable them to see for themselves what God says about His salvation plan.

Eternal Life And Everlasting Life
QUESTION #1203

Is there any textual reason for the King James translators to have used "*eternal life*" in John 3:15 and "*everlasting life*" in John 3:16 when the underlying Greek words seem to be the same in both verses?

ANSWER #1203

You are correct, there is no difference in the Greek text. I think the translators just wanted to vary the phrasing in English to say the same thing in two different ways. Some of the criticisms of the King James Bible have been that many times they translated the same Greek Word in several different ways, depending on the context. This is proper as long as the terms used fall within the permissible meanings.   Eternal and Everlasting life is the result of God's salvation.

How Can The Heathen Be Saved?
QUESTION #1204

How can a person be saved who lives in the Amazon jungle and has never heard of Jesus or seen a Bible?

ANSWER #1204

The clear answer as to how a person can be saved is clear from God's **special revelation** in the Bible. They must genuinely trust the LORD Jesus Christ as their Saviour by faith.

God's **general revelation** in His creation is given in Romans 1:19-20.

> "*Because that which may be known of God is manifest in them; for God hath shewed it unto*

them. 20 **For the invisible things of him** **from the creation of the world are clearly** **seen, being understood by the things that** **are made, even his eternal power and** **Godhead**; so that they are without excuse:"

If they somehow heed God's "*invisible things of Him from the creation of the world*," God might graciously receive them as He did before the Lord Jesus Christ came into the world and died for the sins of the world. It must be left in God's hands. We must keep using God's clear answer in every way possible, and leave the unclear answer to the Lord Himself.

Being Sure As A True Christian?

QUESTION #1205

How can I be sure I am saved?

ANSWER #1205

Thank you for your letter to me about your doubt concerning your spiritual status as to whether you are (1) lost and unsaved, or (2) saved, but carnal and following your sinful flesh rather than the Holy Spirit. Only the Lord knows which of these two possibilities is true.

I.   If you are lost and unsaved, you should sincerely do this:

1.   Agree with God and the Bible that in His sight you are a sinner and lost for all eternity.

2.   Agree with God and the Bible that the Lord Jesus Christ carried and bore all of your sins when He died on the cross of Calvary.

3.   Then genuinely and truly believe on this Saviour as your own and trust His Words in John 3:16 and many other verses which tell you that if your faith in the Saviour is true and genuine, then God grants you everlasting and eternal life.

II. If you are saved, but are living a carnal life after your flesh, you must go to 1 John 1:9 and understand what it means.

1 John 1:9 "*If we confess our sins, he is* *faithful and just to forgive us our sins, and to* *cleanse us from all unrighteousness.*"

The word, "confess" in Greek is HOMOLOGEO which comes from HOMO (same) and LOGEO (to say). It means to say the same thing about our sins as God says and agree that what we have thought, said, done, or where we have gone is sin. If we agree with God about our sins, He promises to be faithful and just to forgive us (because the Lord Jesus Christ paid for all of our sins at Calvary) and to cleanse us from all unrighteousness.

True Christians should practice 1 John 1:9 the minute they sin in thought, word, or deed. Then and only then can fellowship with the Lord Jesus Christ be restored.

Only you and the Lord, know which category you are in: #1 above or #2 above. If you want to talk to me about this, you can call me at either my office (856-854-4747) or on my cell phone (856-261-9018).

The Dean Burgon Society And Salvation

QUESTION #1206

I was looking over the Dean Burgon Society articles of faith here: http://www.deanburgonsociety.org/DBS_Society/articles.htm
I just wanted to understand about the article on "salvation."

"We believe that salvation accomplished by Christ is experienced only through the regenerating power of the Holy Spirit by the Word of God, not by works, but by God's sovereign grace through personal faith in the Lord Jesus Christ as Saviour."

That it allows for the following:

a) Both advocates of what is called "Lordship salvation" and what is called "Free Grace" theology could be DBS members (as long as they agreed to everything else in the doctrinal statement, of course)
and:

b) Both Calvinists and Arminians could be DBS members (as long as they agreed to everything else in the doctrinal statement).

ANSWER #1206

From the Dean Burgon Society's Doctrinal Statement item "G":

"SALVATION"

"We believe that salvation accomplished by Christ is experienced only through the regenerating power of the Holy Spirit by the Word of God, not by works, but by God's sovereign grace through personal faith in the Lord Jesus Christ as Saviour."

In answer to your questions:

In item a), though *"free grace theology"* is not defined, the above Dean Burgon Society's doctrine of "SALVATION" is totally and completely opposed to *"Lordship Salvation."* b) Those who believe in this as defined by John MacArthur and others could not honestly be either "Calvinists" or "Arminians."

Who Are Saved In The Tribulation?
QUESTION #1207

I find myself not really agreeing with the teaching on 2 Thessalonians 2:9-12. I don't think that those who have heard the gospel message before the Tribulation have no opportunity to turn to the Lord during that time to be saved. Is this position wrong?

ANSWER #1207

There are some who take your position, but the section that I, and many others use, is 2 Thessalonians 2:9-12. The Antichrist and Satan will deceive those in the Tribulation and send them "*strong delusion, that they should believe a lie.*" They will not receive the Lord Jesus Christ as their Saviour. But "*they all*" will "*be damned who believed not the truth.*" These are the verses that I, and many others who believe as I do, rest upon.

You and others can take a different interpretation on these verses if you wish, of course. What do the verses mean if they don't mean that these Tribulation people will "*believe a lie*" and "*be damned who believed not the truth*"?

>   **2 Thessalonians 2:9** "*Even him, whose coming is after the working of Satan with all power and signs and lying wonders,*"
>   **2 Thessalonians 2:10** "*And with all deceivableness of unrighteousness in them that perish; because they received not the love of the truth, that they might be saved.*"
>   **2 Thessalonians 2:11**   "*And for this cause God shall send them **strong delusion, that they should believe a lie**:*"
>   **2 Thessalonians 2:12** "*That **they all might be damned who believed not the truth**, but had pleasure in unrighteousness.*"

Lordship Salvation Not Bible Truth
QUESTION #1208

I am looking at the word repentance. I believe in Lordship salvation. Jesus is my Saviour and my Lord. I have no righteousness of my own for I am clothed in the Lord Jesus Christ's righteousness. But the Holy Bible tell us to repent. There seem to be altering views on what repentance means. Some say it means a changing of the mind toward sin but not necessarily turning from our sins. And they talk about the work of the Holy Spirit working in our lives so we will recognize our sins and turn away from them. And I do agree with this as well. What is your opinion on repentance and Lordship salvation?

ANSWER #1208

I'll have to disagree with you on some of this. For example, I am strongly opposed to "Lordship salvation" if you define it as John MacArthur and others define it. That is, he heretically teaches that a person must make Jesus Christ the "Lord" of your life before you can be saved! This is impossible. I am convinced that the Bible clearly teaches the very opposite, that is "salvation Lordship." That is, after a person genuinely receives the Lord Jesus Christ as their Saviour, then and only then, can you and should you make Christ the Lord and Master of your life. It is totally impossible to make the Lord Jesus Christ LORD before you are genuinely saved and born-again! This is blatant heresy!

The Greek Word for "repentance" is METANOIA. It comes from META ("a change") and NOIA from NOUS ("the mind"). It means a change of a person's mind regarding at least three things: (1) a change of mind concerning their sin, that is, an admission that they're sinners in the sight of God and destined to Hell; (2) a change of mind regarding the Lord Jesus Christ, that is, that He died for their sins on the cross; (3) a change of mind regarding the need to genuinely receive the Lord Jesus Christ as their Saviour.

It's obvious that once (and only then) that this change of mind has been accomplished can, should, and must people begin to change their lifestyle and their wicked, sinful habits to conform to the Biblical standards. These are the views that I preach in my church.

CHAPTER II
QUESTIONS ABOUT
THE LORD JESUS CHRIST

Some Of Christ's Blood In Heaven
QUESTION #1209
Hebrews 12:24   *"And to Jesus the mediator of the new covenant, and to **the blood of sprinkling**, that speaketh better things than that of Abel."*

In Hebrews 12:24, was the atonement completed at the Cross or did the blood need to be on the mercy seat in Heaven before the atonement was completed?

ANSWER #1209
That's a good question. In Hebrews 22-24, there are a number of things that are in Heaven. Verse 24 includes "***the blood of sprinkling***." When the Lord Jesus Christ said "*It is finished*" while on the cross, the payment for the sins of the world was accomplished and finished. His placement of some of His blood on the mercy seat in Heaven showed the acceptance of that finished work by God the Father. This took place as our Great High Priest assumed His position at the Father's right hand.

Christ's Atonement
QUESTION #1210
What do you think of this view about Christ's atonement?
"The Work Of Christ" By Paige Patterson
"Regarding the extent of the atonement, the question must be answered: Did Christ die only for the elect, hence, a limited atonement or particular redemption; or did He die for all people, hence, a universal or general atonement? Clearly, the benefits of the atonement are applicable only to those who trust Christ, and those who trust Christ are obviously the ones who are the elect, since no other would come. All evangelical theologians can affirm that

Jesus died 'sufficiently for all but efficiently for the elect.' Furthermore, all evangelicals limit the atonement in some manner. Otherwise, one would of necessity, be driven to universalism. Interestingly, uncertainty exists as to whether Calvin himself believed in particular redemption. . . . The idea of an atonement limited only to the elect is a concept that belongs to a logical system including other elements, such as irresistible grace, which many find appealing. . . . Effectual calling is a more biblical concept, but it should be maintained that God's calling of the elect to salvation does not infringe on the responsibility of sinners to repent and believe the gospel . . . . The atonement of Christ is universal in scope but applicable only for those who receive him (John 1:10-12). It is universal or unlimited in its provision but limited in its application. It is sufficient for all but efficient only for those who believe, who are the elect of God" (Paige Patterson, "The Work of Christ," in A Theology for the Church. ed. Daniel Akin, pages 584-586).

ANSWER #1210

I disagree with many ways Patterson states his hyper-Calvinist ideas about the work of the Lord Jesus Christ. This article is trying to make hyper-Calvinism acceptable to his readers. His use of John 1:10-12 is all right, but the entire article should not be phrased in this strange and contradictory way in order to accommodate his readers to accept his hyper-Calvinism. It should be phrased very simply:

1. The Lord Jesus Christ died for the sins of the whole world (John 3:16).

2. This position does not teach universalism. It does not mean that the whole world becomes a genuine Christian by Christ's death.

3. Everyone in the world is offered this salvation and eternal life, but they can only receive eternal life and salvation if they exercise, from their hearts, genuine faith in the Lord Jesus Christ (John 3:16)

The Temptation Of Christ
QUESTION #1211

Hebrews 4:15 says: *"For we have not an high priest which cannot be touched with the feeling of our infirmities; but was in all points*

tempted like as we are, yet without sin. "
Does this mean that the Lord Jesus Christ had infirmities, or just that
He could sympathize with our infirmities?

ANSWER #1211

The Lord Jesus Christ did not have any infirmities. He was
sinless. But, having seen the various infirmities of many of the
people, He could sympathize with their infirmities though not having
any of His own. Because of His incarnation, and becoming perfect
God and perfect Man, He was able to understand and to sympathize
with human beings.

Faith Is Personal Not By Election

QUESTION #1212

I will be airing this video to the world this fall on TV. Please let
me know if you see any error with any verse of correction of the
prophetic word in the video.

ANSWER #1212

I listened to your video as you requested. You might not believe
in Calvinism, but on this point, you are agreeing with Calvinism. You
are misinterpreting Ephesians 2:8-9. *"For by grace are ye saved
through faith; and **that** not of yourselves: it is the gift of God:"* The
Greek Word for *"that"* is TOUTO. This is in the neuter gender. It is
not in the feminine gender. *"Faith"* is feminine and *"that"* does not
refer to faith. It refers to the verb, SESOSMENE, which refers to the
entire concept of salvation. It is salvation that is not of yourselves.
It is salvation that is not of works. It is salvation that is the gift of
God. Ephesians 2:9 is quite clear that "salvation" is *"not of works,
lest any man should boast."*

Faith <u>In</u> Christ, Not <u>Of</u> Christ

QUESTION #1213

I don't believe in Calvinism, but Jesus is the Author of the
sinner's faith, that not of ourselves, lest we should boast and deny His
one faith given. The Apostle Paul wrote:

> **Galatians 2:16** *"Knowing that a man is
> not justified by the works of the law, but **by the
> faith of Jesus Christ**, even we have believed
> in Jesus Christ, that we might be justified **by
> the faith of Christ**, and not by the works of
> the law: for by the works of the law shall no
> flesh be justified."*

ANSWER #1213

It seems like you are stressing the hyper-Calvinist position that is the faith of Christ that saves (that is, Christ's faith). This seems like you believe that Christ's faith is given only to the elect. In the Greek language, the genitive case of the word, "of" has two meanings: (1) it can be either the objective genitive, or (2) it can be the subjective genitive. I believe it is clearly a use of the objective genitive, meaning faith IN CHRIST, rather than a subjective genitive, meaning Christ's faith. The false subjective interpretation is held by the hyper-Calvinists. They make the same error that is often made in the understanding of Philippians 3:9 where"*faith of Christ*" occurs as well.

The Nature Of Christ's Blood
QUESTION #1214

Although I agree with you that Jesus Christ's blood was Divine blood, I'm not sure how I would defend that position with Scripture. God is Spirit, and Jesus Christ took on human flesh, yet human flesh needs blood to stay alive.

ANSWER #1214

Here are some of the Bible verses that show that the blood of the Lord Jesus Christ was "Divine" that is, prepared Divinely by God the Father.

1.   It is implied in 1 Peter 1:18-19 that His blood was "INCORRUPTIBLE."

> **1 Peter 1:18-19** " *Forasmuch as ye know that ye were **not redeemed with corruptible things**, as silver and gold, from your vain conversation received by tradition from your fathers; **But with the precious blood of Christ**, as of a lamb without blemish and without spot:*"

If people are not redeemed with corruptible things, but with the blood of Christ, it is implied that the blood of Christ is not corruptible, but incorruptible.

2.   It is implied that saved people have been purchased with God's "*own blood*," that is, the blood had its source with God and was Divine in that sense.

> **Acts 20:28**   "*Take heed therefore unto yourselves, and to all the flock, over the which the Holy Ghost hath made you overseers, to feed the **church of God**, which he hath **purchased***

__with his own blood__."
Christ's blood was God's "*own blood*" in the sense that the source of it was from God Himself.

3.   God the Father had to do something other than the blood of animals to take away sin. Therefore He created a special body including special blood.

> **Hebrews 10:4-5** "*For it is not possible that the blood of bulls and of goats should take away sins. Wherefore when he cometh into the world, he saith, __Sacrifice and offering thou wouldest not, but a body hast thou prepared me__:*"

a.   Through the miracle of the incarnation and the virgin birth of the Lord Jesus Christ, Adam's corrupt and sinful blood was not passed on to the Lord Jesus Christ. Sound medical opinion has stated that the blood of a child comes from the father, not the mother. Since the Lord Jesus Christ had no human father, He escaped Adam's sinful blood line.

b.   **Hebrew 10:4-5** Part of verse 5 is a prayer from God the Son to God the Father.

> **Hebrews 10:4** " For it is not possible that the blood of bulls and of goats should take away sins."

> **Hebrews 10:5** "Wherefore when he cometh into the world, he saith, Sacrifice and offering thou wouldest not, but **a body hast thou prepared me**:"

The Lord Jesus Christ mentioned in prayer to God the Father that **"*a body hast Thou prepared Me*."** These verses make it crystal clear that every part of the Lord Jesus Christ's body was "*prepared*" by God the Father and was therefore Divine. This "prepared" body included the Lord Jesus Christ's hands, feet, head, brain, arms, lungs, chest, nervous system, blood, and all of the other thousands of the many parts of the "*prepared*" body of the Lord Jesus Christ.

4.   When a person dies, if he is embalmed, the undertaker removes the blood of the person, because the blood is very corrupt and odorous. Because the blood of the Lord Jesus Christ was special and from God the Father, though He was not embalmed, His body did not corrupt, even during the three days and three nights He was in the tomb.

> **Psalms 16:10** "*For thou wilt not leave my soul in hell; __neither wilt thou suffer thine Holy One to see corruption__.*"

> **Acts 2:27** *"Because thou wilt not leave my soul in hell, **neither wilt thou suffer thine Holy One to see corruption**."*
>
> **Acts 13:35** *"Wherefore he saith also in another psalm, **Thou shalt not suffer thine Holy One to see corruption**."*
>
> *"***Acts 13:36-37** *For David, after he had served his own generation by the will of God, fell on sleep, and was laid unto his fathers, and saw corruption: But **he, whom God raised again, saw no corruption**."*

The reason that the body of the Lord Jesus Christ *"saw no corruption"* was because He did not have the human blood through the line of Adam, but His blood that was from God and thus Divine.

The foregoing are some of the main reasons why I believe strongly that the blood of the Lord Jesus Christ was special, from God the Father, and incorruptible. His blood was far, far different from the blood of bulls or goats, and different even from our own "human blood." Yet John MacArthur heretically referred to Christ's blood as being merely *"human blood"*!

Christ--God's Only Begotten Son
QUESTION #1215

> **John 3:16** *"For God so loved the world, that he gave his **only begotten Son**, that whosoever believeth in him should not perish, but have everlasting life."*

Is *"only begotten Son"* the same as translating it "uniquely related"? In the footnote 3b (of the *Defined King James Bible*) you have used *"Uniquely related."*

ANSWER #1215

It is clear that the Greek Word, MONOGENES is properly translated *"only begotten"* and not *"uniquely related."* This Word shows the proper relationship between God the Father and God the Son by means of the miraculous virgin birth of Christ.

Jesus Is Not The "New Israel"
QUESTION #1216

Is it theologically right to say that: Jesus is the new Israel?

ANSWER #1216

I don't think it is theologically right to say the Lord Jesus Christ is the *"new Israel."* He is not Israel. Israel is a group of people that

God has chosen who will one day return to Him and receive the Lord Jesus Christ as their Saviour.

Jesus Is Not The "New Adam"

QUESTION #1217

Is it Biblically right to say that: Jesus is the "new Adam"?

ANSWER #1217

It is unscriptural to refer to the Lord Jesus Christ as the "*new Adam.*" The only title given to the Lord Jesus Christ regarding Adam is in 1 Corinthians 15:45 where He is called "*the last Adam.*"

> **1 Corinthians 15:45**   "*And so it is written, The first man Adam was made a living soul; **the last Adam** was made a quickening spirit.*"

Christ's Return In The Rapture

QUESTION #1218

I am considering starting a KJV-only Home Bible study, and we may use your service streaming if I can't find anyone around here who can rightly divide the Word of God. I am an RN and Certified Nurse Midwife, and I use the King James Bible in all my midwife books available on Amazon.com. I had been wavering on the pre- and post-Tribulation Rapture views after 25 years of being a pre-Tribulation Rapture believer, but I think I will go back to the pre-Tribulation position after talking with you while preparing for the worst.

ANSWER #1218

You certainly may use our streaming video services in any way you wish. You can also publish them on your possible KJB Home Bible Study or on your Facebook page so long as the proper credits are given. I'm glad you have decided to move back to the pre-Tribulation Rapture position. The 70th week of Daniel must be for "*thy people,*" referring to the Jewish people, not the Gentiles or the church. The church of the Lord Jesus Christ does not have any part in this.

Verses On Wrath From Which
God Delivers True Christians

Romans 5:9 "*Much more then, being now justified by his blood, we shall be **saved from wrath** through him.*" (**not only the wrath of Hell, but the wrath of the Tribulation**).

1 Thessalonians 1:10 *"And to wait for his Son from heaven, whom he raised from the dead, even Jesus, which **delivered us from the wrath to come**."* (not only the wrath of Hell, but the wrath of the Tribulation).

1 Thessalonians 5:9 *"For **God hath not appointed us to wrath**, but to obtain salvation by our Lord Jesus Christ."* (not only the wrath of Hell, but the wrath of the Tribulation).

Revelation 6:16 *"And said to the mountains and rocks, Fall on us, and hide us from the face of him that sitteth on the throne, and from the **wrath** of the Lamb:"* (The saved Christians won't have to hide from His wrath. They will be delivered from it.)

Revelation 6:17 *"For the great day of his **wrath** is come; and who shall be able to stand?"* (The saved Christians are delivered from this wrath).

Revelation 11:18 *"And the nations were angry, and thy **wrath** is come, and the time of the dead, that they should be judged, and that thou shouldest give reward unto thy servants the prophets, and to the saints, and them that fear thy name, small and great; and shouldest destroy them which destroy the earth."* (Christians are delivered from this wrath).

Revelation 14:10 *"The same shall drink of the wine of the **wrath** of God, which is poured out without mixture into the cup of his indignation; and he shall be tormented with fire and brimstone in the presence of the holy angels, and in the presence of the Lamb:"* (Christians will be delivered from God's wrath).

Revelation 14:19 *"And the angel thrust in his sickle into the earth, and gathered the vine of the earth, and cast it into the great winepress of the **wrath** of God."* (Christians are delivered from this wrath).

Revelation 15:1 *"And I saw another sign in heaven, great and marvellous, seven angels having the seven last plagues; for in them is* *filled up the **wrath** of God.*" (Christians are delivered from this wrath).

Revelation 15:7 *"And one of the four beasts gave unto the seven angels seven golden vials full of the **wrath** of God, who liveth for ever and ever.* " (Christians are delivered from this wrath).

Revelation 16:1 *"And I heard a great voice out of the temple saying to the seven angels, Go your ways, and pour out the vials of the **wrath** of God upon the earth.*" (Christians are delivered from this wrath).

Revelation 16:19 *"And the great city was divided into three parts, and the cities of the nations fell: and great Babylon came in remembrance before God, to give unto her the cup of the wine of the fierceness of his **wrath**.*" (Christians are delivered from God's wrath).

Revelation 19:15 *"And out of his mouth goeth a sharp sword, that with it he should smite the nations: and he shall rule them with a rod of iron: and he treadeth the winepress of the fierceness and **wrath** of Almighty God.*" (Christians are delivered from God's wrath).

Verses Showing The Tribulation Is The Seventieth Week of Daniel And For Israel

Daniel 9:24 *"Seventy weeks are determined upon **thy people** and upon thy holy city, to finish the transgression, and to make an end of sins, and to make reconciliation for iniquity, and to bring in everlasting righteousness, and to seal up the vision and prophecy, and to anoint the most Holy.*"

Daniel 9:25 *"Know therefore and understand, that from the going forth of the commandment to restore and to build Jerusalem unto the Messiah the Prince shall be seven weeks, and threescore and two weeks: the street shall be built again, and the wall, even in troublous times.*"

Daniel 9:26 *"And after threescore and two weeks shall Messiah be cut off, but not for himself: and the people of the prince that shall* come shall destroy the city and the sanctuary; and the end thereof shall be with a flood, and unto the end of the war desolations are determined."

Daniel 9:27 *"And he shall confirm the covenant with many for one week: and in the midst of the week he shall cause the sacrifice and the oblation to cease, and for the overspreading of abominations he shall make it desolate, even until the consummation, and that determined shall be poured upon the desolate."*

Apostate Views Of Christ
QUESTION #1219
Is it theologically or Biblically right to think of Jesus or view Him in a "post-metaphysical Christology"? I'd appreciate if you'd explain this term for me!
http://www.amazon.com/Desire-Gift-Recognition-Christology-Postmodern/dp/080286371X
ANSWER #1219
From the LINK that you cited, I would be totally against this desire to view the Lord Jesus Christ in a *"post-metaphysical Christology."* I would stay completely away from anything other than a straightforward literal view of the Lord Jesus Christ as spoken about in the New Testament. None of the doctrines about the Lord Jesus Christ should ever be changed by *"metaphysics"* or anything else. That includes (1) His virgin birth, (2) His miracles, (3) His deity, (4) His perfect humanity, (5) His sinlessness, (6) His omniscience, (7) His omnipotence, (8) His omnipresence, (9) His sacrificial death on the cross for all people who ever lived, (10) His bodily resurrection, (11) His being seated at the right hand of God the Father, (12) His return in the Rapture, (13) His victory at the Battle of Armageddon, (14) His return to earth to set up His reign for 1,000 years in the Millennium,(15) and all the other things about Him that are clearly taught to us in the New Testament.

Hyper-Calvinism's Errors On Christ
QUESTION #1220
Also, what do you consider non-hyper Calvinism on Christ?
ANSWER #1220
I consider "non-hyper Calvinism" of those who agree with the Bible on these three principles: (1) that the Lord Jesus Christ died for

the sins of the entire world, not just some small "elect" group; (2) that whosoever truly trusts and receives the Lord Jesus Christ as their Saviour can receive His promise of not perishing and possessing everlasting life (John 3:16).

Christ's Return At The Rapture

QUESTION #1221

I want to know your stand on the Rapture issue. Our church that I belong to teaches the pre-Tribulation Rapture of all true Christians, but after reading a lot myself, I found this to be false. I believe it should be post-Tribulation and pre-wrath Rapture of the saved Christians. Can you share your views on this issue?

ANSWER #1221

As for disputing your post-Tribulation and/or pre-wrath Rapture position, let me give you some clear Bible verses proving the pre-Tribulation Rapture of all genuine born-again Christians to meet the Lord Jesus Christ in the air according to 1 Thessalonians 4:17. Let me give some verses that pertain to this subject.

> **1 Thessalonians 4:15** *"For this we say unto you by the word of the Lord, that we which are alive and remain unto the coming of the Lord shall not prevent them which are asleep."*
>
> **1 Thessalonians 4:16** *"For the Lord himself shall descend from heaven with a shout, with the voice of the archangel, and with the trump of God: and the dead in Christ shall rise first:"*
>
> **1 Thessalonians 4:17** *"Then we which are alive and remain shall be caught up together with them in the clouds, to meet the Lord in the air: and so shall we ever be with the Lord."*

If your church holds to the pre-Tribulation Rapture of all true Christians, I would agree with them rather than with the books you might have been reading which disagree with that position.

As you may know, there are at least 6 positions on the Rapture of the genuine Christians:

(1) No Rapture at all
(2) Pre-Tribulation Rapture
(3) Mid-Tribulation Rapture
(4) Pre-Wrath Rapture
(5) Post-Tribulation Rapture
(6) Partial Rapture of only some Christians

It is up to you to find a Biblical position on this.

Here are some of my personal reasons for the Pre-Tribulation Biblical position.

REASON #1--THE 70 WEEKS OF DANIEL ARE EXCLUSIVELY FOR ISRAEL AND ARE NOT FOR THOSE CHRISTIANS IN THE BODY OF CHRIST. This is crystal clear in Daniel 9:24.

> **Daniel 9:24** *"Seventy weeks are determined upon thy people and upon thy holy city, to finish the transgression, and to make an end of sins, and to make reconciliation for iniquity, and to bring in everlasting righteousness, and to seal up the vision and prophecy, and to anoint the most Holy."*

REASON #2--THE TRUE CHRISTIANS HAVE BEEN PROMISED DELIVERANCE FROM ALL WRATH, INCLUDING THE WRATH OF THE TRIBULATION. There are two main future "wraths" that the unsaved, lost people living at the time will have to face:

(1) The wrath of the seven-year Tribulation period

(2) The wrath of an eternal lake of fire in Hell

The verse below (1 Thessalonians 1:10) teaches very clearly that genuine Christians are promised to be "**delivered**" from any "**wrath to come**" including the Tribulation wrath.

> **1 Thessalonians 1:10** *"And to wait for his Son from heaven, whom he raised from the dead, even **Jesus, which delivered us from the wrath to come**."*

REASON #3--WHEN RIGHTLY INTERPRETED, THERE IS NO CONTRADICTION WITH THE PRE-TRIBULATION RAPTURE IN 2 THESSALONIANS 2:2-3. I have included part of my coming commentary on 1 & 2 Thessalonians where I explain two views on these verses, both of which would teach the Pre-Tribulation Rapture rather than some other view held by many based on these verses.

> **2 Thessalonians 2:2** *"That ye be not soon shaken in mind, or be troubled, neither by spirit, nor by word, nor by letter as from us, as that the day of Christ is at hand."*

> **2 Thessalonians 2:3** *"Let no man deceive you by any means: for **that day shall not come**, except there come **a falling away**"*

**first**, and that man of sin be revealed, the son of perdition;"

The clause, _"let no man deceive you,"_ is in Greek aorist tense. It is a prohibition. Being in that Greek aorist tense, it means not even to begin this action of deception. If it were a Greek present tense prohibition, it would mean to stop an action already in progress. Paul did not want the genuine Christians in Thessalonica to even begin to have any deception of any kind about this.

You'll notice that _"that day shall not come"_ is in italics and has been added by the King James Bible translators to bring out the sense. If these words make sense, there are two possible conclusions that might be drawn about the meaning of the Word, APOSTASIA, which is used here.

(1) _"That day"_ could refer to the day of the "Lord" Jesus Christ with the apostasy and departure from Bible truths that will occur, followed by the Tribulation period and the revealing of the man of sin, the son of perdition, concluding with the judgment by the Lord Jesus Christ of His enemies at the battle of Armageddon.

Or (2) _"That day"_ might refer to the Rapture of all true Christians if that Word for _"falling away"_ (APOSTASIA) would be understood to mean _"departure."_ APOSTASIA comes from two Greek Words, APO (_"from"_ or _"away"_) and STASIA from HISTEMI (to _"stand"_ or to _"place"_) might be understood to be a _"standing away"_ or _"placing away"_ or _"departure."_ The LOGOS Greek Bible Program uses the English words for APOSTASIA, APOSTASION, or APOSTATES as follows: (1) _"abandonment"_; (2) _"divorce"_; or (3) _"desert."_

If a person _"stands away,"_ they would leave. If a person _"abandons"_ a place, they would _"depart"_ from that place. If a person _"divorces"_ a person, they would _"depart"_ from that person. If a person _"deserts"_ a person or a place, they would _"depart"_ from that person or that place.

I'll leave it up to the reader to decide on the details of this matter. What is crystal clear from all the elements of both the Old Testament and the New Testament regarding future prophetic events, the following chronology is clear:

(1) The Lord Jesus Christ will return to remove and snatch away every genuine Christian in the Rapture before any part of the seven-year Tribulation takes place.

(2) There will then be seven years of Tribulation on this earth called _"Daniel's 70th week"_ or _"the time of Jacob's trouble."_

(3) This Tribulation will end at the battle of Armageddon where all the nations of the earth will gather together around Jerusalem to capture it and the Jews who are defending it. This

battle will end when the Lord Jesus Christ comes down from Heaven in the second phase of His second coming, sets His feet on the mount of Olives, and defeats all His enemies.

Either of the interpretations of the Greek Word, APOSTASIA, will harmonize with these prophetic events.

On Christ's Blood In Heaven #2
QUESTION #1222

Do those like yourself who believe as you have stated--regard, or should regard--those who believe and teach not this doctrine, as somewhat falling short of the Gospel of Christ and lack a fruitful understanding of The Doctrine of Christ? Is it heretical to deny your teaching on this?

ANSWER #1222

You have made it quite clear from your first question and from this response that you do not believe some of Christ's blood was put by Him (after His bodily resurrection) on the mercy seat of Heaven.

There is both a "tabernacle" (3 times in Revelation) and a "temple" (13 times in Revelation) mentioned as being in Heaven. Both that "tabernacle" and that "temple" have a mercy seat, like the ones that were on earth. The Heavenly "tabernacle" was given to Moses as the "pattern" that he was to follow in constructing the earthly tabernacle. Here are some verses showing the *"pattern"* of Heaven was to be used in the tabernacle on earth.

> **Exodus 25:9**   *"According to all that I shew thee, **after the pattern of the tabernacle**, and the pattern of all the instruments thereof, even so shall ye make it."*

> **Exodus 25:40** *"And look that thou **make them after their pattern**, which was shewed thee in the mount."*

> **Numbers 8:4** And this work of the candlestick was of beaten gold, unto the shaft thereof, unto the flowers thereof, was beaten work: **according unto the pattern** which the LORD had shewed Moses, so he made the candlestick.

> **Joshua 22:28** "Therefore said we, that it shall be, when they should so say to us or to our generations in time to come, that we may say again, **Behold the pattern of the altar of the LORD**, which our fathers made, not for burnt

offerings, nor for sacrifices; but it is a witness
between us and you."

If God gave a Heavenly "pattern" to follow, why is it not
reasonable for the Lord Jesus Christ, the true Christians' Great High
Priest, to place His blood, as the Lamb of God, on the Heavenly
altar–as the earthly Jewish high priest did with the lamb's blood on
the Day of Atonement?

Those who reject the position that I believe is Biblical, fall into
at least three different classifications:

(1) Some are unbelieving lost people who don't know about
the Bible's teachings and don't care.

(2) Some might be new evangelicals who compromise on
Biblical separation, on Bible versions, on dress, on music, and other
teachings.

(3) Some might call themselves "Fundamentalists" who also
compromise on Biblical separation, on Bible versions, on dress, on
music, and other teachings.

This present Bible position is clear to many of us, but is not as
clear as many other doctrines.   I don't have any particular
terminology or name for those who do not believe this doctrine. God
alone knows their hearts, minds, and Biblical status.

How Christ Came To Earth
QUESTION #1223
1 John 5:6 "***This is he that came by
water and blood, even Jesus Christ; not
by water only, but by water and blood***.
*And it is the Spirit that beareth witness, because
the Spirit is truth.*"

I have been having a discussion on 1 John 5:6. How do you
explain this verse, "*water*" and the "*blood*"?

ANSWER #1223
In John 5:5, I believe the water there might refer to the bag of
water that breaks upon physical birth. To be born-again, a person has
to have a first birth, but then a second birth by God the Holy Spirit.

In 1 John 5:6, possibly the "*water*" could also refer to the fact
that the Lord Jesus Christ was born physically from Mary.

The word, "*blood*" would refer to the Lord Jesus Christ's special
blood, and all the other parts of His body that were "*prepared*" by
God the Father.

Hebrews 10:5 "Wherefore when he cometh into the world, he saith, Sacrifice and offering thou wouldest not, but **a body hast thou prepared me**:"

He had special blood--blood prepared by God Himself, therefore called God's "*own blood.*"

Acts 20:28 "Take heed therefore unto yourselves, and to all the flock, over the which the Holy Ghost hath made you overseers, to feed the **church of God, which he hath purchased with his own blood**."

I believe that the Lord Jesus Christ, through the virgin birth, escaped the sinful blood of Adam, but was given blood derived from God Himself through the virgin birth by God's miracle.

Therefore, it is entirely possible that it was necessary for the Lord Jesus Christ to have a physical birth (water) but also had to have incorruptible and sinless blood which alone could atone for the sins of the world.

Another Rapture Question
QUESTION #1224

I agree with you on all issues, but am undecided on the pre-Tribulation Rapture issue because the church fathers didn't teach it and, I am a student of the Puritans. I was brought up on the pre-Tribulation Rapture position in AWANA, Pensacola A BEKA teachings, and the Scofield Reference Bible. I am still considering this issue.

ANSWER #1224

If you agree with the Puritan leaders:

(1) You must share their unBiblical view of Hyper-Calvinism that Christ did not die for the sins of the whole world, but only for a small group of the "elect."

(2) You must also believe, with them, that "whosoever will may come to Christ" is false and only those who are the "elect" can come to salvation by genuine faith in the Lord Jesus Christ.

(3) According to the Puritan leaders, John 3:16 doesn't mean that God so loved the entire "world" even though it says so, but just a small group of "the elect."

(4) You and the Puritan leaders would have a giant chasm between what you believe about God and His salvation, and what we believe the Bible teaches on these matters.

Calvin Against Biblical Christology

QUESTION #1225

I have studied John Calvin. He persecuted true believers because they would not baptize their children. His followers would also go and drag people out from their houses and make them go to church. I wanted to know if you have any resources against Calvin and his wrong doctrines.

ANSWER #1225

Calvinists have followed many heretical teachings on the Lord Jesus Christ including His death on the cross for the elect only, and their belief that only the elect could become true Christians rather than whoever truly trusts the Lord Jesus Christ.

For many articles against some of the views of John Calvin and the Calvinists, you may go to the LINK below and search for Calvin articles.

http://biblefortoday.org/idx_Pages/idx_catalog.htm   Look for "*Calvinism and Election.*" You'll find over 25 articles on this subject there.

More On Christ's Blood

QUESTION #1226

Can you give me some information on the blood of Christ, especially about putting some of it on the mercy seat in Heaven?

ANSWER #1226

Thank you for your email about the message by another speaker on the Blood of Christ. Let me answer your question as follows:

1.   By the pastor's saying that the work of the Lord Jesus Christ on the cross "*was not enough*" (or "*not complete*"), he was not diminishing or minimizing that work on the cross. It was not complete in two areas:

(1) There had to be His bodily resurrection to authenticate God the Father's acceptance of that death as payment for the sins of the world.

(2) Secondly, there had to be the placing of some of His blood on the mercy seat of Heaven. Many of us believe this also had to be done for Christ's work to be complete.

There are many (like John MacArthur, John Walvoord, and many others, perhaps you, and some of your friends) who do not believe that the Lord Jesus Christ, after His bodily resurrection, returned to Heaven and placed some of His blood on Heaven's mercy seat, as the true Christians' Great High Priest and as the custom of the earthly priests was to complete the offering on the Day of Atonement (Leviticus 16:14-15). I, however, (along with many other Bible-believing Christians and leaders), believe that the Lord Jesus Christ did place some of His blood on the mercy seat of Heaven right after His bodily resurrection in completion of His work on the cross. The timing of this event is found in John 20:17:

> **John 20:17** *"Jesus saith unto her, Touch me not; for **I am not yet ascended to my Father**: but go to my brethren, and say unto them, I ascend unto my Father, and your Father; and to my God, and your God."*

This verse tells us when the Lord Jesus Christ "*ascended*" to God the Father to accomplish this. Here are some verses that show His Blood is in Heaven:

> **Hebrews 9:12** "Neither by the blood of goats and calves, but **by his own blood he entered in once into the holy place**, having obtained eternal redemption for us."

The Lord Jesus Christ, the Christians' Great High Priest, did not take the blood of goats and calves to the holy place of Heaven, but He took "*His own blood*" there.

> **Hebrews 12:22** *"But ye are come unto mount Sion, and unto the city of the living God, the heavenly Jerusalem, and to an innumerable company of angels,"*
>
> **Hebrews 12:23** *"To the general assembly and church of the firstborn, which are written in heaven, and to God the Judge of all, and to the spirits of just men made perfect,"*
>
> **Hebrews 12:24** "And to Jesus the mediator of the new covenant, **and to the blood of sprinkling**, that speaketh better things than that of Abel."

Of all of the things mentioned in these verses that are in Heaven, "***the blood of sprinkling***" is included. This is a reference to the Blood of the Lord Jesus Christ.

2.   In saying that work of the Lord Jesus Christ on the cross "*was not enough*" is correct. Though I understand what was meant by the term, I wouldn't have used the term "*that's no good*." I would have said that "*It was not complete*."

What you believe about: (1) the bodily resurrection of the Lord Jesus Christ (2) His putting some of His blood on the mercy seat in Heaven--determines whether or not you would agree that Christ's work on the cross "*wasn't enough*" and "*wasn't complete.*" These are the reasons why I said I agreed with the message of that speaker.

CHAPTER III
QUESTIONS ABOUT
THE KING JAMES BIBLE

King James Bible Is Not "Inspired"
QUESTION #1227

Since Dr. Jack Moorman believes in the inspiration of Scripture, and since the King James Bible claims to be Scripture, and since it would make no sense to inspire something that you were going to judge this world by, without preserving it—do you now become of one mind and one mouth with us that believe the King James Bible is the inspired and preserved Word of God? And farther, why would Satan, the god of this world, spend so much time counterfeiting it, by changing it, if it wasn't the Word of God which is inspired and preserved to judge this world by, including him?

ANSWER #1227

No, God did not breathe out or inspire the King James Bible. It is therefore not God-breathed or inspired. This view that you hold is heresy. Though this heretical view is held by the Peter Ruckman and Gail Riplinger followers, it is still very untrue. The King James Bible was translated by well-equipped and skilled translators from 1604 to 1611. It is the only accurate English translation of the God-breathed, inspired, and preserved original Words of Hebrew, Aramaic, and Greek.   Only the Hebrew, Aramaic, and Greek Words are God-breathed and inspired.

The Meaning Of Bible Inspiration
QUESTION #1228

Job 32:8 says: *"But there is a spirit in man: and the inspiration of the Almighty giveth them understanding."*

I don't know why you can't see it. You have a blindness over your heart. Because of it, you are missing out on many understandings just like the Jewish people. You say the word inspiration means *"God breathed,"* yet that is not in the Bible. He preserved it as *"inspiration."*

You limit God as if He can only inspire the original manuscripts, which no one has, and that He can't inspire any thing today. He isn't using or calling the originals His word, but does in no uncertain terms call the King James Bible His inspired word. That is what he is referring to, to this generation. The English will give more light and understanding, than the Hebrew or the Greek.

ANSWER #1228
You are uninformed and dead wrong in denying that "inspiration" means "God-breathed."

> **2 Timothy 3:16** *"All scripture is **given by inspiration of God**, and is profitable for doctrine, for reproof, for correction, for instruction in righteousness:"*

The five words in the King James Bible in 2 Timothy 3:16, *"given by inspiration of God"* is the translation of one Greek Word, THEOPNEUSTOS. This Greek Word comes from two Greek Words, THEOS ("God") and PNEUSTOS from PNEO ("to breathe"). Taken together, it means "God-breathed."

If you take the heretical position that the King James Bible is "inspired" by God, which one of the 7 editions of the King James Bible do you think God *"inspired or breathed out"*? Edition #1, #2, #3, #4, #5, #6, or #7? If God "inspired" it, did He make a mistake in edition #1, #2, #3, #4, #5, #6, so He had to make edition #7? Also, why are you charging our God for including the 12 to 14 books of the Apocrypha in the 1611 first edition? The Apocrypha contradicts the Bible in many places. Are you accusing our God in making such contradictions? You can continue to follow your heretical friends, Peter Ruckman, Gail Riplinger, and their followers if you wish. But I will maintain truth and strongly reject this error and heresy.

The King James Bible's Origin
QUESTION #1229
What would you recommend to me as an introductory source about the King James Bible, and how it came into being?

ANSWER #1229
I think that the best introductory beginning source of the study of the King James Bible would be my own book, *DEFENDING THE KING JAMES BIBLE--A FOURFOLD SUPERIORITY.* (**BFT #1594 @ $15.00 + $5.00 S&H**). I believe it sets the stage for this important topic. In the Appendix of this book, there are several hundred more titles on this theme. We also list many other books on

this subject in the BFT Catalog found at the LINK below:
http://biblefortoday.org/idx_Pages/idx_catalog.htm

King James Bible And The LXX
QUESTION #1230
Did the King James Bible translators use the Septuagint (LXX)?
ANSWER #1230
The King James Bible translators made reference to the LXX in their *"Preface to the Readers,"* but we do not have to agree with their views of the LXX. We stand for their excellent translation of the Hebrew, Aramaic, and Greek into English. There is no evidence to show that they used the LXX in any way in their King James Bible translation. They relied solely for their textual bases on the Hebrew, Aramaic, and Greek Words. Though others differ on this, I believe the LXX originated with Origen (184-284 A.D.). It was his 5th column of his 6-column Hexapla Bible. Evidence indicates that the LXX was not in existence as an entire unit B.C. It originated A.D.

The AV, KJV, AND KJB NAMES
QUESTION #1231
What is the difference, if any, between the "Authorized Version," the "King James Version," and the "King James Bible"?
ANSWER #1231
The Authorized Version, the King James Version, and (what I prefer) King James Bible, all refer generally to the same thing. The original Authorized Version of 1611 has been updated in spelling and in a few other things as of 1769. This is the seventh edition that was used by the Cambridge University Press. It is the version we use in our *Defined King James Bible.* The versions taken from the Oxford University Press (like the Old Scofield Reference Bible) have about 100 to 150 places where they wrongly depart from the Cambridge University Press readings.

Changes In The King James Bible
QUESTION #1232
Why are there various changes in the different editions of the King James Versions?
ANSWER #1232
It is true that the so-called "King James Versions" published by Zondervan, Moody, Kregel and other publishers differ in many places from our *Defined King James Bible* and other Bibles published by the Cambridge University Press. Here is the reason for this. When the

Authorized Version was published in 1611, and in later editions, in England, it had a kind of copyright called "*cum privilegio.*" As such, neither the Cambridge University Press nor the Oxford University Press could alter it in any way. When the United States began to print the King James Version, they refused to be bound by "*cum privilegio*" or any other copyright rules. Because of this, these publishers are able to change their King James Versions any way they wish. For example, in the spelling of names. They wrongly change Elias to Elijah. They wrongly change Jeremy to Jeremiah. They wrongly change Isaias to Isaiah. They make many other changes, however slight, throughout their translations as well, and wrongly claim their "translations" to be "The King James Version."

Where Was 1 Corinthians Written?
QUESTION #1233

Some Bible commentators say that the King James Bible is wrong when it says that the 1 Corinthian letter was written from Philippi. They say it was written from Ephesus. What is your opinion in regard to the alleged claim of the King James Bible?

ANSWER #1233

1.   Though the footnote at the end of 1 Corinthians in the 1611 King James Bible stated this, there are many King James Bibles that have no such editorial ending.

2.   The location where the books of the New Testament were written cannot be certainly ascertained. There are various answers.

3.   Such additions to the 1611 King James Bible, as well as some of the comments in the "*Translators To The Readers,*" are not part of their translation of the Bible books. These opinions do not need to be agreed to, since they are not a part of their accurate translation of the Bible books.

The King James Bible With Tenses
QUESTION #1234

Can you recommend a King James Bible with the Hebrew and Greek tenses in them?

ANSWER #1234

For the Hebrew or Greek Words used for the English, *Strong's Exhaustive Concordance* has these in the appendix. For the tenses used, I would recommend that you get the Logos Bible Software program. Their software gives every part of speech, tense, meaning, and forms used for both Hebrew and Greek.

Large KJB In Red Ink
QUESTION #1235
I would like to buy an Authorized King James Version Bible large letter Bible, with the words of the Lord Jesus in red.

ANSWER #1235
We do not have our *Defined King James Bibles* in red and black ink for several reasons: (1) the cost would be very high; (2) older people's eyes make it more difficult for them to read red ink easily; (3) all of God's Words are important, not just those spoken by the Lord Jesus Christ, or by God the Father; and (4) It is often not clear whether or not God the Father or the Lord Jesus Christ is speaking, leading to an uncertainty as to which words should be in red ink.

You can check http://biblefortoday.org/kj_bibles.asp to see the cost and size of our *Defined King James Bible*. You can either order online or can call **856-854-4452** with your credit card and order by phone.

Errors Of King James-Onlyism
QUESTION #1236
What does this sentence mean? *"I haven't been King James Only for a decade now."*

ANSWER #1236
The person who wrote this probably meant that he no longer believes the King James Bible was the **ONLY** thing we are to use or make reference to in Bible study. This heresy believes the Words that God gave us in Hebrew, Aramaic, and Greek have all been replaced by their false belief that the King James Bible was a second inspired document that replaces the Hebrew, Aramaic, and Greek Words. He probably means that he now has returned to the truth and now believes that the Hebrew, Aramaic, and Greek Words that underlie the King James Bible can be consulted for further understanding. The heretical "King James Only" heresy has been held and promulgated by Peter Ruckman, Gail Riplinger, and their many followers.

Inspiration And Preservation
QUESTION #1237

In your opinion, what were the errors in my pastor's Sunday message on "*The Bible's Preservation And Inspiration*"?

ANSWER #1237

Let me give you the following comments about this sermon you sent me which your pastor preached on a recent Sunday morning:

1. I'm glad he has gone verse-by-verse through 12 or 16 books of the Bible in the last 12 years as your pastor.

2.   He promised not to change your church's doctrinal statement about the King James Bible, but promised to keep the King James Bible. I question the sincerity, validity, and duration of that promise. It seems like in time, after you and others like you die, he might go back on that promise and change Bible versions.

3. I notice he's reading most of his message. He has it written down and possibly will publish this in a book when his series is complete.

4.   He quotes correctly the Greek Word for "*given by inspiration of God*" (THEOPNEUSTOS), but this inspiration refers only to the original Hebrew, Aramaic, and Greek Words and accurate copies of those original Hebrew, Aramaic, and Greek Words, yet he wrongly and heretically uses it to apply to the King James Bible or other versions. At the end of his talk, he held up his King James Bible and said this is the "*inspired, preserved Word of God.*" This is pure heresy! No version is "*inspired*" or "God-breathed"! To say the King James Bible is inspired shows that your pastor is a follower of the heresies of Peter Ruckman, Gail Riplinger, and their many followers.

5.   The list of his 10 books is totally one-sided. I don't remember all of them, but (1) *From the Mind of God to the Mind of Man* stands in favor of the Gnostic Critical Greek Text, as do (2) John Ankerberg's materials, (3) Comfort's materials, (4) James White's materials, and probably the others that I don't remember. The only sound, sane, and sensible book he cited which stands for the Traditional Greek N.T. Text is (5) my book, *Defending The King James Bible*. He omitted entirely all 13 books by Dr. Jack Moorman and all the 5 books of Dean John William Burgon plus many others who hold to the Textus Receptus Greek New Testament and the proper Hebrew, Aramaic, and Greek Words as well. This shows his bibliography to be totally unbalanced and will end him up on the wrong side of the textual issues.

6. He was correct that there are around 5,500 copies of various parts of the Greek New Testament today.

7. He didn't want to get into the solid fact that Westcott and/or Hort were members of the Ghostly Guild which communicated with dead people. He couldn't bring himself to speak anything against Westcott and Hort whom he loves, admires, and follows slavishly as to their preferred texts (which will be seen in his later messages).

8. At one point he heretically referred to the writers of the Bible as *"inspired authors."* They were not *"inspired"* or *"God-breathed."* The Words which King James translators translated from the Hebrew, Aramaic, and Greek originals were the only Ones that were given by God the Holy Spirit. They were the only *"inspired and God-breathed Words"* which are or every will be in existence.

9. He's right when he said there is no "re-inspiration." It occurred once and was never repeated once the Bible was completed in 90 or 100 A.D.

10. He's right that we don't have the autographs, but we do have hundreds of copies of the autographs. By comparing these copies, we can discern what the original Words were . The problem he is going to have with these copies, is to determine which Words--taken together--form the exact Words of the original autographs. I believe those original, preserved Hebrew, Aramaic, and Greek Words are the Words from which the King James Bible was accurately translated into English. Your pastor will say that the false Words found in the Gnostic Critical Text of Westcott and Hort, Nestle-Aland, and The United Bible Societies Greek texts are the proper Greek New Testament Texts to use. This text is founded on merely around 45 Greek New Testament manuscripts that follow the many Vatican and Sinai false Gnostic readings.

11. He is in error when he said that God had His hand in all translations of the Bible! Those taken from the wrong Hebrew, Aramaic, or Greek Words are totally false from the very beginning.

12. He is in error when he said "*You read the **Divine Words** when you read your Bible.*" Which Bible is he referring to? Though the words of the King James Bible are accurate translations of the proper Hebrew, Aramaic, and Greek Words, the English words are not "*Divine Words*"! They are accurate **translations** of the "*Divine Words*"!

What Is KJB "Inspiration Light"?

QUESTION #1238

What is your definition of "*inspiration light*"? I have heard you use that term in the audio messages but did not grasp a precise meaning.

ANSWER #1238

I know of former leaders in our Dean Burgon Society who have left it because of their belief (contrary to the standard of the Dean Burgon Society's Doctrinal Statement) in using the term "*inspiration*" for the King James Bible saying that it is in some way "*inspired*," however "*light inspiration*" is implied.   This is heresy. This is explained more fully in the DBS Questionnaire which every DBS leader must believe and sign each year. It explains the heresy of the King James Bible partaking of "*inspiration light*" which some of our former DBS leaders used to modify "*inspiration*":

> [*NOTE*: Neither the King James Bible or any other language translation, will be referred to as "*inspired*" in any sense at all, including "*derivative inspiration*," "*indirect inspiration*," "*having the mark of inspiration*," "*inspired in a 'generic' or general sense*" or any other similar terms that might be brought up to modify "inspired" or "inspiration."]

Only the Hebrew, Aramaic, and Greek Words were inspired or God-breathed by God.   The King James Bible is an accurate translation of the inspired and God-breathed Hebrew, Aramaic, and Greek Words that God gave us.

Many heretically believe that the King James Bible has "*inspiration heavy*." This includes Peter Ruckman, Gail Riplinger, and their many followers. They believe that God gave people a second revelation and a re-inspiration in the English language called the King James Bible. As such, they teach that what God actually gave us in Hebrew, Aramaic, and Greek Words are not to be consulted, but to be thrown out and completely replaced with the English translation of the King James Bible. This view is also heresy–far greater than the "*inspiration light*" heresy–but both are heresies, whether light or heavy.

KJB Pre-Critical Text?
QUESTION #1239
Is it all right to say that: "the King James Bible's New Testament was based on a "pre-critical Greek text"? What does "pre-critical Greek text" mean in this case?
ANSWER #1239
The King James Bible is based upon the Traditional Greek Text which pre-dated the Gnostic Critical Greek Text of 1881. Perhaps that's what is meant by the "pre-critical text." It was largely taken from Theodore Beza's Greek Text of **1598**. The Gnostic Critical Greek Text of Westcott and Hort, Nestle-Aland, and the United Bible Societies were published from **1881** A.D. and beyond. These false Greek Texts are based largely on the 4th Century A.D. Vatican and Sinai Greek Manuscripts. Though the Vatican and Sinai sources were early, the publication of the false Greek Texts occurred almost 400 years after the true and accurate Traditional Greek Text was in print.

King James And The KJB
QUESTION #1240
Thanks be to Almighty God for the Authorized Version of Holy Scripture. I find it to be tragic that King James I has his name appended to the Authorized Version of Holy Scripture. Why is this? I do believe, like yourself, that the Authorized Version is the only true, reliable, and accurate English translation of the original, inspired, inerrant, infallible, preserved Hebrew, Aramaic, and Greek Words that underlie it.
ANSWER #1240
As you may know, the title for the King James Bible in the early days was the Authorized Version, because it was authorized by King James. He had nothing to do with the actual translating process and procedure. His name has been linked to the Authorized Version because he is the one who authorized it.

Original KJB Drawings
QUESTION #1241
What do you think of this message on the KJV in ths LINK from the Cutting Edge? http://www.cuttingedge.org/news/k1002.cfm
ANSWER #1241
I am against what the Cutting Edge people are doing to oppose the King James Bible. The translators of the King James Bible did not necessarily believe in these drawings that appeared in their

original printed Bible. These drawings might have been inserted by the masons that lived in 1611. The printers of the original KJB put all these pagan pictures and other things in the original KJB which were not necessarily believed by the King James Bible translators at all. I have seen the Cutting Edge people smearing the KJB in this way before.

Gipp, Ruckman, And Riplinger

QUESTION #1242

What do you know of Samuel Gipp? Is he a credible defender of the King James Bible?

ANSWER #1242

Samuel Gipp cannot be trusted in the King James Bible battle which is raging today. Gipp graduated from Peter Ruckman's Pensacola Bible Institute. He holds the same heretical position on the King James Bible as Peter Ruckman held. He believes God performed another breathing-out (THEOPNEUSTOS) or inspiring of His Words in the King James Bible rather than limiting inspiration and God's breathing-out His Words exclusively in the Hebrew, Aramaic, and Greek Words underlying the King James Bible. In addition to this, Gipp and Ruckman might possibly now go along with Gail Riplinger's even more heretical position when she says we should throw away God's Hebrew, Aramaic, and Greek Words underlying the King James Bible. She heretically believes that God gave a special inspiration and God-breathing of the English words of the King James Bible. Since she believes this lie, she advocates that we should throw away all the Hebrew, Aramaic, and Greek Words and make no reference to them. She wants everyone to limit their Bible to the English of the King James Bible. This position is pure and total heresy thought up and pushed by this unBiblical woman preacher. Her false theories should be avoided completely!

KJB's Formal Equivalency

QUESTION #1243

1. Are we using a term that has no existence in reality when we refer to "*formal equivalency*"?

2. When God quotes in the New Testament verses in the Old Testament, why are there slight changes?

ANSWER #1243

1. Dean Burgon's definition of "*formal equivalency*" means that where possible, the "forms" of the Hebrew, Aramaic, and Greek Words should not be changed. That is, nouns should be translated as

nouns, adjectives as adjectives, verbs as verbs, and so on. Literal word-for-word translating often would make no sense. "*Verbal equivalency*" should occur in translations. Wherever possible, every form of the Words of the original languages should be accurately translated into the same form of the word in the translation in question.

Word-for-word translation is an entirely different subject. There cannot be such literally, because the rules of grammar differ from the Hebrew, Aramaic, and Greek languages to English, Spanish, French, or other languages. For example, it would be folly, according to our English rules of grammar to translate word-for-word John 1:2. The Greek order is KAI THEOS EN HO LOGOS. The Greek says "and GOD was the Word." Our English grammar puts the subject first, "And the Word was God." Word order many times changes with various languages as well as other factors. This doesn't give us an excuse to either add words, subtract words, or change words in some other way. All the words must be accurately translated. Our KJB translators used italics when they felt it would help our English language make clear what the Hebrew, Aramaic, or Greek grammar meant by their syntax.

2. Regarding Old Testament quotations in the New Testament, it is true that often there is a difference. I maintain that the Lord Jesus Christ gave the Words to God the Holy Spirit, and the Holy Spirit gave the Words to the human writers of both the Old Testament and the New Testament.

> **John 16:12**   "*I have yet many things to say unto you, but ye cannot bear them now.*"
>
> **John 16:13**   "*Howbeit when he, the Spirit of truth, is come, he will guide you into all truth: for he shall not speak of himself; but whatsoever he shall hear, that shall he speak: and he will shew you things to come.*"
>
> **John 16:14**   "*He shall glorify me: for he shall receive of mine, and shall shew it unto you.*"
>
> **John 16:15**   "*All things that the Father hath are mine: therefore said I, that he shall take of mine, and shall shew it unto you.*"

Because of this, the Lord Jesus Christ had a reason to alter some of the Words in order to suit His own purposes when bringing over verses from the Old Testament into the New Testament context. When I write a book or an article, as the author, I have a right to change it, alter it, add to it, subtract from it when using it in different contexts. That doesn't mean that my first wording was wrong. It merely means that my purposes in using these words are different. As the original author, I have every right to change my idea in any way I might wish for the new purposes that I have in the new context.

Bible Preservation Of Words

QUESTION #1244

Psalms 12:6 *"The words of the LORD are pure words: as silver tried in a furnace of earth, purified seven times."*

Psalms 12:7 *"Thou shalt keep **them** O LORD, thou shalt preserve **them** from this generation for ever."*

Regarding these verses above some have referred *"them"* to the people rather than the Words of the Bible. Which is correct?

ANSWER #1244

Dr. Jack Moorman, one of our church's missionaries in England, has a good analysis of these two verses mentioned above (**BFT #2524   52 pp. $5.00 + $3.00 S&H** *Psalm 12:6-7 And Bible Preservation* By Dr. Jack Moorman.) Though the New International Version and some of the other Bible translation perversions refer the *"preserve them"* to people, the context is crystal clear that God is referring to *"the words of the LORD"* that He will keep and preserve.

CHAPTER IV
QUESTIONS ABOUT
THE HEBREW AND GREEK TEXTS

The Proper Hebrew Text
QUESTION #1245

It is very difficult for me to find good offline sources of information on significant differences between the ben Asher Masoretic Text and the ben Chayyim Masoretic Text. Could you please point me to some good online sources?

ANSWER #1245

I do not know of any online sources for this. Nor do I not know of any off-line study that has compared the Ben Chayyim Hebrew with the Ben Asher Hebrew text. I have been seeking documentation on this for over 40 years. One man began it, but quit. The Trinitarian Bible Society leaders in London, England, told me there were just a few differences. I don't believe that, however.

When Rudolph Kittel compiled his Hebrew text, he used the Ben Chayyim text in his 1906 and 1912 editions. Then, in 1937, his successors changed to the Ben Asher Hebrew Text. This was also used in the Hebrew Stuttgart edition. It seems to me that there had to be a sufficient reason in order to institute this expensive replacement Hebrew text. If there were only "*a few differences*" between these two editions, this would not explain to me the reasons for this change. As to the actual differences, I'm sorry that no one has come up with them as yet. I know for certain in Isaiah 9:3, (cited below), the ben Asher Hebrew Text has removed the "*not*" from the ben Chayyim Hebrew Text. Sorry that I cannot be more definitive for you in your good question.

> "*Thou hast multiplied the nation, and **not** increased the joy: they joy before thee according to the joy in harvest, and as men rejoice when they divide the spoil.*" (Isaiah 9:3)

Masoretic And Received Texts
QUESTION #1246
Could you please help me (a novice) in a sentence or two to understand the relationship of the Masoretic and "Received" texts?
ANSWER #1246
The Masoretic Text is the traditional Hebrew text that has been "received" of the Old Testament Scriptures. The Beza 1598 is the Traditional Greek text that has been "received" of the New Testament Scriptures. There are other New Testament "received" texts, but I believe the Beza is the closest to the preserved original Greek Words.

Proper Hebrew And Greek Texts
QUESTION #1247
Where can we find the accurate Masoretic Hebrew and Textus Receptus Greek?
ANSWER #1247
The Hebrew/English Text
BFT #2064, 1384 pages, $85.00, *Hebrew Masoretic O.T. Underlying The King James Bible With The KJB Parallel*, Edited By Ben Chayyim, published by the American Bible Society (The price might be higher now.)
The Textus Receptus Greek Text
We carry two editions of this Greek Text:

BFT #471, $18.00 + $8.00 S&H, 487 pages, *The Greek New Testament, The--Received Text*; published by the Trinitarian Bible Society Staff.

BFT #1670, $38.00 + $10.00 S&H, 668 pages, Scrivener's Annotated Greek New Testament With T.R. & W & H Text Made Clear, By Dr. Frederick Scrivener, published by the Bible For Today.

False Manuscripts For New Bibles
QUESTION #1248
If the new Bible documents only have small portions available, how do they come up with a complete Bible?
ANSWER #1248
Though there are some manuscripts that contain just some verses or chapters, there are many that are more complete which cover verses and chapters that others leave out. The result is that all of the Words of God have been preserved when comparing all of the some 5,500 New Testament manuscripts that God has preserved for us. The new Bibles are based on manuscripts which follow the

heretical Gnostic Critical texts of the Vatican and Sinai documents. There are only about 45 manuscripts used by these false versions (less than 1% of the total), whereas the King James Bible is based on over 99% of the manuscript total–over 5,210.

Biblical Criticism

QUESTION #1249

What does textual criticism deal with?

ANSWER #1249

Biblical criticism is usually divided into two major areas. Textual criticism is called *"lower criticism."* It deals with determining the original Hebrew, Aramaic, and Greek Words of the Bible. *"Higher criticism"* involves determining the authorship and dates of the various Bible books.

The Hebrew Roots Movement

QUESTION #1250

A neighbor of mine is into the Hebrew Roots Movement. He says that the New Testament was originally written in Hebrew and only later in Greek. Is he correct or wrong?

ANSWER #1250

Your friend is wrong. His is an unproven theory. If the New Testament were originally written in Hebrew, there would be thousands of New Testament Hebrew manuscripts. This is not the case. There are more than 5,500 Greek manuscripts that have been preserved. It is clear that God used Hebrew and Aramaic in the writing of the Old Testament. He used the Greek language for the writing of the New Testament.

The Dates Of Corrupt Greek MSS

QUESTION #1251

Where is the proof that any of the corrupt manuscripts date back to around 325 A.D.?

ANSWER #1251

The dates of the corrupt Gnostic Critical Text Sinai and Vatican manuscripts are have been estimated at around 350 or 375 A.D. There are no dates on them, but that is the conclusion both sides have agreed upon. Dean Burgon found that the Sinai and Vatican MSS differed from each other in at least 3,000 places in the Gospels alone!

Dr. Jack Moorman's book on *8,000 Differences Between The Critical Text And The Textus Receptus* (**BFT #3084 @ $29.00 + $10.00 S&H**) lists each one of the 8,000 differences. 356 of these differences involve doctrinal passages. His book on *Early Manuscripts, Church Fathers and The Authorized Version* (**BFT #3230 @ $20.00 + $10.00 S&H**) lists each of the 356 doctrinal passages with the Greek manuscripts supporting the truth and those supporting the errors.

Antiochian vs. Alexandrian MSS
QUESTION #1252
Antioch Greek Texts versus the Alexandrian Greek texts. Here is an 8-minute video explaining the differences. What do you think of the video below?

https://www.youtube.com/watch?v=SoQ39VPjzoc
ANSWER #1252
This is only a brief 6-minute video, but it is very helpful. It shows the superiority of the Greek manuscripts from Antioch and the inferiority of the Greek manuscripts from Alexandria.

2ND Year Greek Grammars
QUESTION #1253
I feel the need to make a comment about the book you use for the second-year Greek course. The authors favor the Westcott and Hort Greek text. Why do you recommend and use that book?
ANSWER #1253
I'm glad you bought Dana and Mantey's book. Perhaps it is a new edition of the book. Mine is dated 1959 and does not have any such praise of the Westcott and Hort false Greek text. I realize that they followed A. T. Robertson's large Greek Grammar and they used the false Gnostic Critical Texts used by Westcott and Hort, Nestle-Aland, and the United Bible Societies. The reason I use Dana and Mantey in 2nd year Greek is not because of their false Greek text, but because of their excellent summary of the various Greek tenses and uses that are found in very few other Intermediate Greek Grammars.

If you want to know and understand the Greek language, you should want to know all of these grammatical details. Forget what New Testament Greek Text these men believed in. That's not the point in studying Greek grammar! A. T. Robertson's over 1,000-page large grammar book is excellent in Greek grammar, regardless of the false New Testament Greek text he wrongly uses. It is sad to say, but those who stand for the Greek Textus Receptus as I do, have not written any exhaustive Greek grammars. For study, we must rely on those with whom we differ and be very cautious in using their books.

If you can find an excellent intermediate Greek Grammar whose author or authors stand for the Textus Receptus and the King James Bible as I do, let me know and I can recommend it. Otherwise, you have two choices: (1) Use Dana and Mantey's *Intermediate Greek Grammar* to study the meanings of the Greek language; or (2) Give up your exhaustive study of the many rules of Greek grammar altogether and not be able to fully understand the various meanings of the Greek New Testament that underlies the King James Bible..

Original New Testament Language
QUESTION #1254
One of the church fathers records that Matthew wrote in Aramaic. Is this true?
ANSWER #1254
I don't agree with the argument that many espouse that Matthew, or any other part of the New Testament, was originally written in Aramaic. It was written in Greek. We have over 5,500 Greek manuscripts of the New Testament. There are very, very few Aramaic New Testament manuscripts which would not be true if the New Testament was written in Aramaic.

Bible Preservation Is Biblical
QUESTION #1255
Matthew 5:18 *"For verily I say unto you, Till heaven and earth pass, **one jot or one tittle** shall in no wise pass from the law, till all be fulfilled."*

I was using Matthew 5:18 to prove a point and someone said "the expression jot or tittle" doesn't appear anywhere in the Greek New Testament, in any variant. I have not been able to find an answer to this. Is there an article or book that addresses this?
ANSWER #1255
Whoever told you this is either totally ignorant of the Greek text, or had a mental breakdown at some point and forgot to look it up again. The King James Bible Word for "*jot*" is a translation of the Greek Word, IOTA. That is the smallest letter in the Greek language. The King James Bible Word for "*tittle*" is a translation of the Greek Word, KEREIA. That is a punctuation mark which is just a dot ("."). The Lord Jesus Christ has promised to preserve His Hebrew, Aramaic, and Greek Words not only including the books, the chapters, the verses, the words, but also the very smallest letters. These same two Greek Words occur in my copy of the Nestle-Aland

Gnostic Critical Greek Text. I'm sure they are found in the United Bible Societies Gnostic Critical Greek Text. I'm also sure they are found in the Westcott-Hort Gnostic Critical Text that I was given to study at Dallas Theological Seminary. I don't know if there is an article or a book on this, but such is not needed in this case.

The Gnostic Greek Texts
QUESTION #1256
Why do you refer to the Nestle-Aland, United Bible Societies, and Westcott and Hort Greek texts as "Gnostic"?
ANSWER #1256
The Nestle-Aland, the United Bible Societies, and the Westcott & Hort Greek texts follow the Gnostic heretical doctrines in 356 places as listed by Dr. Jack Moorman in his book, *Early MSS, Church Fathers, and the Authorized Version* (**BFT #3230 @ $20.00 + $8.00 S&H**). Alexandria, Egypt, was the headquarters of the Gnostic Religion. It was also the source of both the Vatican (B) and the Sinai (Aleph) Greek Manuscripts which were altered into Gnostic doctrines in 356 passages. This makes them Gnostic manuscripts.

Masoretic Hebrew And TR Greek
QUESTION #1257
What is a good book giving the background of the Masoretic Hebrew and the Textus Receptus Greek texts?
ANSWER #1257
For a book that tells about the Masoretic Hebrew Text and the Textus Receptus Greek Text background and history, I suggest Dr. Jack Moorman's book, *Forever Settled* It is **BFT #1428 @ $20.00 + $10.00 S&H**. That would be an excellent start on this venture.

Manuscripts TR vs. Critical Text
QUESTION #1258
Since the manuscripts supporting the King James Bible outnumber those supporting the new versions (over 99 percent to less than 1 percent), shouldn't the new versions' translators borrow from the King James Bible manuscripts in order to complete the translations of their Bibles?
ANSWER #1258
What the translators from the Gnostic Critical Greek Text do is just to translate from their Gnostic Critical Greek New Testament manuscripts and leave out, add, or change in some other way whatever Words are found in our Traditional Received Greek Words

that underlie our King James Bible. Because of this method, Dr. Jack Moorman has documented over *8,000 Differences Between The Gnostic Critical Greek Text and our Received Greek Text.* (**BFT #3084 @ $29.00 + $8.00 S&H**). Though some of these Greek changes are not noticed in the translation, he has specified over 356 doctrinal passages that are involved in these Gnostic Critical Greek Texts of the New Testament. This is very serious indeed.

Translation Of Hebrew Words
QUESTION #1259

I have a Bible question. Someone mentioned during a meeting that some Hebrew words cannot be translated into English. Can you explain what this person meant? I really didn't know how to respond to his comment.

ANSWER #1259

That statement is false. Every Old Testament Hebrew Word and every New Testament Greek Word can be translated into English. Each of those original Words have 3 to 5 shades of meaning in English. The King James Bible translators selected one of these various meanings and placed it in the King James Bible. Perhaps this person was referring to the few number of Hebrew Words which were used only once in the Bible. This is called a *hapax legomenon.* To properly translate these Words, our King James Bible translators went to the cognate or sister languages which used those words where the meanings were known. They then assigned these meanings to translate those Hebrew Words.

CHAPTER V
QUESTIONS ABOUT
OTHER BIBLE VERSIONS

The Paraphrased Bible
QUESTION #1260

What is your opinion about saying "A paraphrased Bible is better than no Bible? In my opinion, it would be best just to eliminate that kind of statement. A little leaven leaveneth the whole lump, and these perversions are leaven.

ANSWER #1260

The right Bible, properly translated into the person's language, is the best, of course. However, a person may be living in a country with no accurately-translated Bible available, (as is true in many nations of the world). Much as we would differ with such a paraphrased translation, a Bible with some salvation truths that would enable a person to get saved, would be better than for the person never to read any of these verses at any time during his or her lifetime then be lost and go to Hell forever.

The Old Latin Bible
QUESTION #1261

Greetings from Southwestern Ontario, Canada, in the precious and worthy name of the Lord Jesus. I am hoping you can give me some direction regarding a few matters of research.

I am looking for a translation in English of the Vetus Itala (The Old Latin Bible). This would be a translation put in book form of all the extant manuscripts, being especially interested in any predating the Vaticanus and Sinaiticus or quotations from church Fathers (so-called).

Which translation of the Syriac Peshitto into English would you suggest is more accurate?

ANSWER #1261

Here are a few LINKS that might help to answer these questions for you:

THE OLD LATIN (VETUS ITALA)

http://vulgate.net/ (on the *Vetus Itala* Old Latin to be put on the computer some time)

http://en.wikipedia.org/wiki/Vetus_Latina (on the Old Latin, background and possible printed sources)

http://www.vetuslatina.org/ (resources as to where to get the Old Latin)

THE SYRIAC PESHITTA

http://en.wikipedia.org/wiki/Peshitta (about it)

http://www.peshitta.org/ (an interlinear translation with Aramaic)

The Geneva Bible

QUESTION #1262

Is the Geneva Bible just as inerrant as the King James Bible 1611?

ANSWER #1262

First of all, I do not use the word, "*inerrant*" for the King James Bible. I consider it to be "*accurate*" and a "*careful*" translation, but anything that man put his hand to cannot be called "*inerrant.*" Only God can produce things like the Hebrew, Aramaic, and Greek Words of the Old and New Testaments that are "*inerrant.*"

Regarding the Geneva Bible, it was based on the same Hebrew, Aramaic, and Greek Words as the King James Bible, but it is not as accurate as the King James Bible. John Bois, one of the translators of the King James Bible, asked if King James would authorize another Bible translation; he mentioned the reason for this need—he said, "*the versions extant* (in existence) *not answering to the originals.*" In other words, these other versions (including the Geneva Bible (1560) which was then in existence) were not as accurately translated as they should be. I have not made a verse-by-verse study of the Geneva Bible, but I take this man's word for its not being as accurate as it should be.

Another downside, in my opinion, of the Geneva Bible is that its notes are loaded with John Calvin's theology which is erroneous in many ways. He and his followers, the Calvinists, did not believe the Lord Jesus Christ died for the sins of the whole world, but just for the sins of the elect few.

The Reese Chronological Bible
QUESTION #1263
I have the *Reese Chronological Bible*. I like it so far. What do you think of it compared to the King James Bible?
ANSWER #1263
Although chronology helps, I prefer the King James Bible which goes book by book rather than by dates.

Other Views On Bible Translations
QUESTION #1264
Is there room for other views on the translation of the Bible in addition to those mentioned in this tract that I was reading?
ANSWER #1264
1. The back of the tract you mentioned says that we should examine the "*faithfulness*" of any translation "*to the original languages.*" The problem with translations other than the King James Bible is that they have different Hebrew, Aramaic, or Greek original Words on which they base their translations. They do not use the same Traditional Old Testament Hebrew and Aramaic Words and the Traditional Received Text New Testament Greek Words. This is a very serious difference.

2. The tract talks about "*the test of doctrinal accuracy*" and we are to "*compare the copy to the original.*" If we have different originals, we have different doctrines. The heretical Gnostic Critical Greek New Testament Text changes doctrines in over 356 places. All of these 356 places are listed in Dr. Jack Moorman's book, **BFT #3230** *Early Manuscripts, Church Fathers, And the Authorized Version* @ $20.00 + $10.00 S&H.

3. I do not hold any translation (including the King James Bible) to be "*inspired*" or "*God-breathed.*" I believe this is a serious heretical position taken by Peter Ruckman, Gail Riplinger, and all their followers.

4. Only the "*original, inspired writings*" of Hebrew, Aramaic, and Greek should be the foundation of any translation. These were the basis of the King James Bible, but were not the basis for the modern versions.

5. The latest translation that Bob Jones University favors now is the English Standard Version. They used to favor the New American Standard Version. These two versions as well as the NIV, RSV, NRSV, ASV, and a host of other modern versions have as their Greek New Testament the Gnostic Critical Greek Text.

This corrupt Greek text, (according to Dr. Jack Moorman's large book, *8,000 Differences Between the T.R. and the Critical Text*) [**BFT #3084 @ $29.00 + $8.00 S&H**] has over 8,000 differences in it compared to the New Testament Greek Words underlying the King James Bible. Though many of these 8,000 differences are not great, there are at least 356 passages that are seriously doctrinal in nature. All 356 passages and their false doctrines in the Gnostic Critical Greek Text are listed and explained in almost 200 pages of Dr. Moorman's book *Early Manuscripts, Church Fathers, and the King James Version* (BFT #3230 @ $20.00 + $10.00 S&H) mentioned earlier.

The Dangers Of New Versions
QUESTION #1265

A while back I heard a preacher tell us that he could tear apart any major doctrine using the modern versions. Of course his intent was to prove the dangers of these so-called translations. I am out looking for those verses and translations that would show the dangers, and I hope you just might have such a list. How might I go about getting the list from you, or where do I need to go to get that list? I have been collecting these translations and perversions now for a couple of years, and want to present a lesson or two on the subject.

ANSWER #1265

Dr. Jack Moorman, one of our church's missionaries in London, England, wrote a book that we published called *8,000 Differences Between the Textus Receptus and the Critical Text*. Of the 8,000 differences, there are 356 which are doctrinal passages where these new versions (RSV, NRSV, ASV, NASV, NIV, ESV and all the other English or foreign language versions that are based on the Gnostic Critical Greek N.T. Text) are doctrinally incorrect on all these 356 passages. This book is **BFT #3084 @ $29.00 + $10.00 S&H**.

All 356 doctrinal passages are listed in almost 200 pages of Dr. Moorman's book entitled *Early Manuscripts, Church Fathers, And The King James Version*. It is **BFT #3230 @ $20.00 + $10.00 S&H**. If you really want to see what these 356 doctrinal passages are that are found in these modern translations in English and in all the other languages of the world, I recommend you get this book and see the various doctrines that are either omitted, changed, or challenged. That's where your desired "list" can be found. The Greek Manuscripts defending the proper doctrines are given also.

Bible Versions And Copyright Laws
QUESTION #1266
Am I correct when I say that each version of the Bible has to be different in doctrine in order to get a copyright? If you have something not too long that I could pass along on Facebook regarding this, I'd really appreciate it!
ANSWER #1266
It is not correct to say there must be *"different in doctrine"* to get a copyright. There must be a certain percentage of words that are different. (http://www.answers.com/Q/What_percentage_of_a_written_work_must_change_to_get_a_copyright) The LINK above is helpful in answering this question, although there is no specific percentage given that must be different between the two books.

New King James Version Defects
QUESTION #1267
What are some of the defects in the New King James Version?
ANSWER #1267
In my analysis of the New King James Version from Genesis through Revelation, I found over 2,000 examples of either adding to the Hebrew, Aramaic, or Greek Words, or subtracting from these Words, or changing them in some other way. This is **BFT #1442 @ $15.00 + $10.00 S&H**. These facts make the New King James Version unacceptable for the genuine Christian who really wants to know that all of God's Words have been accurately translated into English--with none of the Words subtracted, none added, and none changed in other ways.

Living Bible Version
QUESTION #1268
Do you have materials exposing the errors of The Living Bible?
ANSWER #1268
Here are some of the materials we have that are against The Living Bible.

BFT #289, Cassette $4.00 + $2.00 S&H *Finding The Needle In The Haystack--Living Bible Exposed* By Dr. D. A. Waite

BFT #86, 6 pages, 2/$2.00 + $1.00 S&H *I wouldn't Dare Treat the Bible That Way!* By Dr. David Otis Fuller

BFT#386, 47 pages, $3.00 + $2.00 S&H, *The King James Version vs. Taylor's Paraphrase*, By Dr. Oliver B. Greene

BFT #199, 92 pages, $4.00 + $2.00 S&H, *The Livid Libel of the Scriptures of Truth*, By Dr. Ian R. K. Paisley

BFT #663, 8 pages, $2.00 + $1.00 S&H, *The Living Bible Critique*, By the Trinitarian Bible Society Staff

BFT #127, 344 pages, 11.00 + $7.00 S&H, *The Paraphrased Perversion of the Bible–The Living Bible*, By Dr. Gene Nowlin

CHAPTER VI
QUESTIONS ABOUT
VARIOUS DOCTRINAL POSITIONS

Anglican Church Doctrines
QUESTION #1269
I am a Bible-believing Christian, who is currently emerging from the deceit of Anglican Church doctrine.   Please see my email communication to a person as well as his response. Can you please address my concerns. I need to know if I've made any errors. Thank you for your assistance, and I look forward to your response at your earliest convenience.
ANSWER #1269
I'm glad you're emerging from the Anglican Church doctrine. I have inserted (at the very, very bottom of this email) an article on "*50 Years of Liberalism in the Anglican Church*" by David Cloud which I think you will enjoy.

Regarding King James, you have no doubt brought out many truths about this King. I have read many who have castigated him in an effort to destroy the effectiveness of the King James Bible. Regardless of all of the stones you can throw at King James--and there are many--one thing is absolutely certain! He had nothing whatever to do with the actual translation of the King James Bible.   He appointed scholars in Hebrew, Aramaic, and Greek. They were the men who translated the King James Bible.   The king gave these translators a few rules to follow, but he did not enter into the translation itself. I don't know what your views are about the King James Bible, but if you want my views, you will find them in my book, *DEFENDING THE KING JAMES BIBLE* (**BFT #1594 @ $15.00 + $8.00 S&H**).

David Jeremiah's Positions
QUESTION #1270

I'm wondering what are your thoughts about Dr. David Jeremiah?

ANSWER #1270

I have mixed feelings regarding David Jeremiah. I know him personally, and I knew his father before him. Mrs. Waite listens to him each Sunday morning on TV. He is a good speaker and says many things we would agree with, despite his use of the New King James Version. He is a graduate of the Dallas Theological Seminary as I am. As such we agree with many of his doctrinal positions. However, I am a Biblical separatist without anything to do with either the National or World Councils of Churches which are apostate, or with the National Association of Evangelicals who work with the apostates. David Jeremiah differs with my position on Biblical separation and fellowships with compromise groups. As such, by his silence on this vital doctrine of the Bible (2 Corinthians 6:14--7:1), he is leading many people into the one world church, whether he knows it or not. I have not followed him in detail. If I did, I'm sure I would find many, many other things where we would disagree on Biblical principles. He does not like me and wrote things against me at one time which were false. Since he is a born-again Christian, I love him in the Lord, but differ strongly with some of his beliefs and practices.

Thomas Strouse's Theology
QUESTION #1271

I was wondering if you knew of Dr. Thomas M. Strouse of Bible Baptist Theological Seminary of Cromwell, CT. If so, is he sound biblically?

ANSWER #1271

Thanks for your note about Bible Baptist Theological Seminary in Cromwell, CT. I have known Dr. Strouse for many years. He used to be part of the leadership of the Dean Burgon Society, but left, because it was not directly out of some local Baptist church.

There are many things I agree with Dr. Strouse on such as: (1) standing for the King James Bible; (2) standing for the Hebrew, Aramaic and Greek Words underlying the King James Bible; (3) separation from apostasy and I think also neo-evangelicalism; (4) the sovereignty and independence of the local Baptist Churches; (5) in his belief in geocentricity as opposed to heliocentricity (the former being denied by many today).

However, the main and strong objections I have with Dr. Strouse are: (1) his limiting of the "Body of Christ" exclusively to his type of a local Baptist church; (2) his denial that even other doctrinally-sound Baptist churches who might differ with him on some points are not in the "Body of Christ"; (3) his belief that the Church began in the Gospels with the apostles (apparently including Judas Iscariot) as the first members of the first Baptist Church; (4) his belief in some kind of secessionism in Baptist churches that goes back to New Testament times; (5) his denial that each and every genuinely born-again and saved Christian is in the *church, Which is His body"* (Ephesians 1:22b-23a) or the Body of Christ, regardless of denominational or non-denominational affiliation.

I'm sure you would receive good training in the Biblical languages and in Old Testament and New Testament Bible, and you might even be persuaded by him on the 5 things above where we differ, or, you might continue to believe what you believe that might be contrary to these 5 points (if he will let you graduate without holding his position). These are just a few thoughts. If you have further questions, give me a call at 856-854-4747, and we can talk about it.

Freemasonry
QUESTION #1272
What are your comments on Freemasonry?
ANSWER #1272
You are right that Masonry is evil and heretical. It is unchristian and even Satanic. Below is a LINK that mentions just a few of the errors of Masonry. No Christian should ever be a part of this evil system, yet many are. Look at this LINK to see these errors.
 http://www.ramministry.org/freemasonry.htm

Paul Carlson's Ministry
QUESTION #1273
My former church is having a big Paul Carlson rally. They are celebrating their fifty years of this organization and Paul Carlson's martyrdom. Please tell me what would you do in this kind of situation. I am willing to be obedient.
ANSWER #1273
If this man was an unbeliever or an apostate in his beliefs, I think you are doing right by not attending this service. The LINK below tells about Paul Carlson in detail. He says there are many contradictions in the Bible. He sounds like an apostate Antichrist.

Stay away from him.
http://infidels.org/library/modern/paul_carlson/nt_cont
radictions.html

The verses below on Biblical Separation are very clear:

2 Corinthians 6:14   *"Be ye not unequally yoked together with unbelievers: for what fellowship hath righteousness with unrighteousness? and what communion hath light with darkness?"*

2 Corinthians 6:15   *"And what concord hath Christ with Belial? or what part hath he that believeth with an infidel?"*

2 Corinthians 6:16   *"And what agreement hath the temple of God with idols? for ye are the temple of the living God; as God hath said, I will dwell in them, and walk in them; and I will be their God, and they shall be my people."*

2 Corinthians 6:17 *"Wherefore come out from among them, and be ye separate, saith the Lord, and touch not the unclean thing; and I will receive you,"*

2 Corinthians 6:18 *"And will be a Father unto you, and ye shall be my sons and daughters, saith the Lord Almighty."*

David Sorenson's Commentaries

QUESTION #1274

I received a packet of newspapers from *The Sword of the Lord*. There was an advertisement that caught my attention. Pastor David Sorenson's *Understanding the Bible* commentaries were the product being advertised. Is this a commentary set that you would recommend?

ANSWER #1274

I have a set of Sorenson's commentaries. I have not looked into them or used them very much. Though he used to speak kindly of me, he now holds me as an enemy. There two things I strongly disagree with him on, though there might be others as well. There are probably many other things we would be in agreement on. The two important things that I know I differ with him about are: (1) He believes it's all right for a person who is the so-called *"innocent party"* to divorce a marriage mate and marry someone else while the mate is still living. I differ strongly with him on this teaching. (2) He believes that the King James Bible is, in some sense of the word, *"inspired."* I believe this to be a serious heresy. I believe that only the original Hebrew, Aramaic, and Greek Words were "*inspired*" or "*God-breathed*" in any sense of the word. The King James Bible is the only accurate English translation of those inspired, God-breathed, original, preserved Words.

Foundations Bible College
QUESTION #1275

Some time ago our church had a preacher come to our country called Dr. Spence from Foundations Bible College in Dunne, South Carolina. Since that time, about 4-5 yrs ago, I have found out some things he believes that concern me. He believes all the gifts in the Bible are available today at the discretion of the Holy Spirit. I would like to know all I can about the source of all this at Foundations Bible College. How do I prove from Scripture that the sign gifts have passed away? Is 1 Corinthians 13 enough?

ANSWER #1275

Thank you for your note and comments on the Foundations Bible College. The following LINK tells about this Bible College.
http://www.foundations.edu/about_fbc/main.php They don't give a detailed doctrinal statement, however.

I understand they were formerly totally Pentecostal and charismatic, but I understand they have changed somewhat. Personally, I would have nothing to do with this Foundations Bible College until they gave me a detailed doctrinal statement of what they believe. The LINK below only gives part of that belief.
http://www.foundations.edu/about_fbc/theological_pers pective.php It is only their "theological perspective." It is not a detailed doctrinal statement at all. You might write them and ask them for this. They might not respond, but you could still request it.

The four verses below from 1 Corinthians 13:8-11 show that these sign gifts such as prophecies, tongues, special knowledge and, by implication, all the other special sign gifts, shall fail, cease, vanish, and be done away. The important question is **when** will this take place? Verse 10 answers the question of **when**.

All these and other of the so-called sign gifts will fail, cease, vanish, and be done away, "***when that which is perfect is come***." The four English words, "***that which is perfect***" are a translation of two Greek Words: TO TELEION. Both in the English ("*that which*") and in the Greek (TO TELEION) are neuter genders. They are neither masculine nor feminine.

Those who twist TO TELEION into a masculine gender are dead wrong! They make it refer to the idea of "*when **He** shall come*" (referring to the second coming of the Lord Jesus Christ. That is completely impossible due to TO TELEION being in the neuter gender. There must be a neuter noun to go with it. I believe it refers to TO BIBLION (the Bible). I believe this refers to the time (about 90 to 100 A.D.) when the entire Bible was made perfect, finished, and completed. That is when I believe all these sign gifts failed, ceased, vanished, and were done away.

> **1 Corinthians 13:8** *"Charity never faileth: but whether there be prophecies, they shall fail; whether there be tongues, they shall cease; whether there be knowledge, it shall vanish away."*

> **1 Corinthians 13:9** *"For we know in part, and we prophesy in part."*

> **1 Corinthians 13:10** *"But when that which is perfect is come, then that which is in part shall be done away."*

> **1 Corinthians 13:11** *"When I was a child, I spake as a child, I understood as a child, I thought as a child: but when I became a man, I put away childish things."*

Andrew Murray Part #1

QUESTION #1276

I am sure you have heard of Andrew Murray. How sound is he in the doctrines of the faith?

ANSWER #1276

http://www.scielo.org.za/pdf/vee/v30n1/15.pdf

The LINK above shows that he believed in Divine healing.

http://bennozuiddam.com/Lee%20on%20Andrew%20Murray.pdf

The LINK above questions whether or not this Dutch Reformed church man is a genuine "Calvinist" or a "Pentecostalist."

http://www.thepathoftruth.com/false-teachers/andrew-murray.htm

The LINK above calls him a "False Teacher" in various areas.

I suggest you look at all three of these LINKS and come to your own conclusions about his beliefs and practices.

Andrew Murray Part #2
QUESTION #1277

What are some of your comments on this long article about Andrew Murray?

http://archive.org/stream/AndrewMurrayAndHisMessage-Upload
edByDavidTurner/AndrewMurry_djvu.txt

ANSWER #1277

Here are some of my comments from the long article above:

1. The writer (I think it's his mother) writes "*from the standpoint of the Dutch Reformed Church of South Africa.*" This may refer to his father or relative, but if it is one of his beliefs, **he would seem like a hyper-Calvinist**.

2. In Chapter XXII, the title is "THE NECESSITY OF THE PENTECOSTAL SPIRIT" (page 308). Unless this refers to his father or a relative, but if it refers to him, **it sounds like he might be "Pentecostal" in some respects**. It might imply the necessity for speaking in tongues as on the Day of Pentecost, etc. Strange position!!

3. From another source, both brothers [Andrew and John] were ordained by the Hague Committee of the Dutch Reformed Church on 9 May 1848. **If he believed the doctrines of the Dutch Reformed Church, he was a hyper-Calvinist thinking Christ died only for a certain few "elect" people, but not for the sins of the world as John 3:16**.

4. From this same other source, "Murray was also a key Higher Life or Keswick leader, and **his theology of faith healing and belief in the continuation of the apostolic gifts made him a significant forerunner of the Pentecostal movement.**" **I consider both these positions in #3 and #4 to be HERESY**! I am sure many things he wrote you might agree with, but with these beliefs, he is DANGEROUS as a theologian to follow.   This is from http://en.wikipedia.org/wiki/Andrew_Murray_%28minister%29 if you want to look it up.

5. "Murray authored over 240 books, including: "**Divine Healing**."

6.   "The Andrew Murray Bible School is run by the Christian Reformed Theological Seminary on the East Rand, an institution that offers inter-denominational theological courses covering a wide spectrum. It offers degree and diploma courses presented in the form of study guides compiled by lecturers who are university-accredited and university-appointed. The student has to work through these study guides on his/her own. The courses of the Andrew Murray Bible School are academically of a very high standard. The Seminary has a

Reformed basis of faith with the emphasis on world evangelization.

John MacArthur

QUESTION #1278

What are your views about John MacArthur?

ANSWER #1278

I disagree with John MacArthur on a number of things. I have written a book against his heresy on the blood of the Lord Jesus Christ.

(1) He denies that "blood" means "blood" but heretically believes that it is only a metonym for "death." The Lord Jesus Christ shed His blood at his death, but "blood" must be taken literally here and not changed to mere "death."

(2) He believes in the heresy of "Lordship salvation" so that people cannot be saved until they first make Jesus "Lord." The Bible teaches salvation first, and then the Lordship of Christ, not the other way around. Unsaved people can never make Jesus "Lord" of their lives until after they become genuine Christians.

(3) He takes the heretical position of hyper-Calvinism which denies that Christ died for the sins of the whole world, but believes He died only for a small number of "elect" people. No one but the elect can believe on the Lord Jesus Christ and be saved, contrary to John 3:16.

(4) He believes the gospel of Jesus in the Gospels is the same gospel mentioned in the epistles.

(5) He believes Christians have only one nature rather than two natures, the flesh and the indwelling Holy Spirit.

(6) There are many other practices of John MacArthur in his neo-evangelicalism and failure to separate from false doctrines or disobedient brethren. He cannot be trusted in his theology regardless of his huge following.

Replacement Theology

QUESTION #1279

I have a relative who is attending a church in which the pastor holds to Replacement Theology. Would Replacement Theology be considered heresy?

ANSWER #1279

Replacement Theology is a very serious heresy, in my judgment. This heresy replaces the nation of Israel with the church today, thereby wiping out the distinction between the church and Israel with all of its promises that God made to Israel in the Old Testament.

Replacement Theology teaches that all these promises to Israel are fulfilled in the church today. This is a serious heresy because it violates the principles of Biblical hermeneutics (interpretation) and does not rightly divide the Words of truth.

Lordship Salvation
QUESTION #1280

Good day! I was looking over the Dean Burgon Society articles of faith here:

http://www.deanburgonsociety.org/DBS_Society/articles.htm

I just wanted to confirm that in the article on "salvation" here:

"We believe that salvation accomplished by Christ is experienced only through the regenerating power of the Holy Spirit by the Word of God, not by works, but by God's sovereign grace through personal faith in the Lord Jesus Christ as Saviour."

That it allows for the following:

a) Both advocates of what is called "Lordship salvation" and what is called "Free Grace" theology could be DBS members (as long as they agreed to everything else in the doctrinal statement, of course).

b) Both Calvinists and Arminians could be DBS members (as long as they agreed to everything else in the doctrinal statement).

ANSWER #1280

"G. SALVATION

We believe that salvation accomplished by Christ is experienced only through the regenerating power of the Holy Spirit by the Word of God, not by works, but by God's sovereign grace through personal faith in the Lord Jesus Christ as Saviour."

In answer to your questions:

a) Though "Free Grace" theology is not defined, the above DBS doctrine of SALVATION is totally and completely opposed to "lordship salvation." Those who believe in this as defined by John MacArthur and others could not honestly sign our DBS doctrinal statement.

b) Our Dean Burgon Society doctrinal statement does not address either "Calvinists" or "Arminians."

Jehovah Witnesses Heresy

QUESTION #1281

The reason for this communication, is because I'm having a dialogue with several Jehovah's Witnesses. They sent me several links to explain this. If you would be so kind, please review these links and tell me what you think. I'd also be interested in your opinion of the Jehovah Witnesses.

ANSWER #1281

Regarding the LINKS you sent about the New World Translation. The first LINK said nothing about the Hebrew, Aramaic, and Greek Texts used for their translation that I could see.

The second LINK was very clear:

"Reliability. The New World Translation is based on up-to-date scholarly research and the most reliable ancient manuscripts. In contrast, the King James Version of 1611 was based on manuscripts that were often less accurate and not as old as those used in producing the New World Translation."

That says it all. Just as their original translation was based on the Gnostic, Critical Greek New Testament texts, so this one brags about their "old" manuscripts (meaning Vatican and Sinai). As such, their New Testament (according to Dr. Jack Moorman's book *8,000 Differences Between the Critical text and the Textus Receptus*, (**BFT #3084 @ $20.00 + $10.00 S&H**) has 8,000 N.T. differences with our T.R. underlying our KJB Greek N.T. Of these 8,000 differences (some of them minor), a total of 356 are DOCTRINAL PASSAGES!

Here's a LINK to a 12-minute video showing the Jehovah's Witnesses New Testament is based on the Vatican manuscript (https://www.youtube.com/watch?v=o1pFppVooEQ).

As for the serious doctrinal perversions and heresies in the Jehovah Witnesses' Cult, here are some items we carry in our Bible For Today store. You might like to get one or more of these:

BFT #272 156 pp. $4.00 Heart To Heart Talks With Jehovah's Witnesses, by Duncan, Rev. H.

BFT #1309 Cassette $4.00 Hour With Cults--Armstrongism; Mormon; Ch.Sci.; JW's by Waite, Dr. D. A.

BFT #862 191pp. $7.00 I Was Raised A Jehovah's Witness by Hewitt, Joe

BFT #2125 110 pp. $11.00 Jehovah's Witnesses And The Person Of Christ by Meadows, Rev. D.

BFT #381 18pp. $1.50 On The Wrong Train by Duncan, H.

BFT #1918 6 pp. 5/$1.50 Reasons (15) Why I Cannot Be A

Jehovah's Witness by Mignrd, Robert.

BFT #1569 64 pp. $6.00 Watch Tower, The--A Field White Unto Harvest by Williamson, Pastor John

Here is a link to the appendix A in our Bible. In A1-A5 it shows how the Bible was translated, the methods used, and some of its features. I think you will enjoy looking at this:

http://wol.jw.org/en/wol/publication/r1/lp-e/nwtsty/E/2015/5

Also here is a book that I have found interesting: *Truth in Translation--Accuracy and Bias in English Translations of the New Testament* by Jason David BeDuhn.

Here's another link to an article you might find interesting:

http://www.jw.org/en/jehovahs-witnesses/faq/new-world-translation-accurate/#?insight[search_id]=ba6eb4c3-a5ed-48fb-87e0-8c1b1d931c33&insight[search_result_index]=37

McClure's And Paine's Books
QUESTION #1282

Is it possible to obtain online PDF versions of the two books that you mentioned?

ANSWER #1282

I don't know of any downloads of these books, but here are their LINKS.

http://www.wilderness-cry.net/bible_study/translators/ tells about McClure's book.

http://www.amazon.com/The-Behind-King-James-Version/dp/0801070082 tells about Paine's book.

CHAPTER VII
QUESTIONS ABOUT
LOCAL CHURCH DECISIONS

Baptismal Regeneration
QUESTION #1283
Does water baptism in a local church save a person's soul?
ANSWER #1283
Water baptism by immersion is only for genuinely born-again Christians in obedience to the Lord's command. It does not save and cannot save the soul. This is a false teaching believed by many today. It is a misinterpretation of Acts 2:28:

> *"Then Peter said unto them, Repent, and be baptized every one of you in the name of Jesus Christ __for__ the remission of sins, and ye shall receive the gift of the Holy Ghost."*

Many people misinterpret the Greek Word, *"for"* which is used in this verse. It does not mean *"in order to receive."* In verse, the Greek words means *"because of."* The proper understanding of this verse is that water baptism should be undertaken only after a person's sins are remitted and they are saved. There are five or six places in the book of Acts where after people became genuine Christians, they were baptized by immersion in water.

Ordination And "Reverend"
QUESTION #1284
What is your position on ordination and the title "Reverend"?
ANSWER #1284
On the use of *"Reverend,"* though I don't prefer it, it is used to designate a man who has been ordained as a minister by a local church. I prefer the title of "Pastor." As for ordination, though it might not be required to serve the Lord as a pastor, I believe it is fitting for a local church to examine a pastoral or missionary candidate as to his conversion, his call to the ministry, and his doctrines. This should determine his initial fitness for being qualified as a pastor or a missionary.

Internet Churches And Communion
QUESTION #1285

In working on Hebrews 10, I would have a question about an Internet church not being able to take Communion, when we are commanded to do so.

On the other hand, I realize the problem there is in people finding a good church nowadays and not wanting to be in the liberal, modernist churches. I drive 3 hours on Sunday to go to two services, which not everyone would be able to do. Even at that, there are things at that church that I don't agree with but can just not participate in it, so separate in that way. I do think fellowship and actually being together are important. Anyway, I thought I'd send along my thoughts on it since I'm in the midst of doing those scriptures on not forsaking the fellowship together.

ANSWER #1285

I believe those who worship with us on our Internet services are "*not forsaking the assembling of themselves*" together with us. I believe they are following the Bible much more literally than those who go to churches that are close to them, but are either liberal, neo-evangelical, or fundamental with things that disagree with the Bible.

I believe you, as others of our Internet family have asked and practice, can take communion with us there in your home and fulfill the 1 Corinthians communion passage in the 21st Century Internet reality.

I admire your 3 hours each Sunday traveling to this church, but as to those who insist on attending **local** churches, it doesn't sound like 3 hours total per Sunday is very **local**. You do as you wish, but we'd be glad to have you as one of our Internet family at our church and your "*assembling yourself together with us*" each Lord's Day and Thursday evening. But you must make this choice. I am not trying to persuade you contrary to your own wishes and will, but you asked me a question, and I tried to do my best to answer it as I believe.

The Lord's Supper
QUESTION #1286

Hello Pastor, please pray as our family is dealing with finding a church. The last church I talked with believes one needs to do the Lord's supper every week. The men who run the church tried to show Scripture to me that if you do not do it each week, you're not following the Lord's commandment. I just felt that something was not correct. This church does use the King James Bible, but they only have a few so-called men to teach. They do not want a pastor. This thinking has kept us from attending. Do you have anything that teaches on the Lord's Supper?

ANSWER #1286

Thanks for your note and request. The church you are attending is probably associated with the Plymouth Brethren group. They do not have pastors. They have several of their elders speak. They usually meet in a circle and only those who are on the inner circle can take communion. The have communion each Sunday.

I don't have any books on this, but I just know that there are groups that have this each week. Others, like our church, have communion each month. There are some groups that have it only four times a year, and there are still other groups that have it only once a year.

I think the verses to remember as to the frequency of the Lord's Table are 1 Corinthians 11:24-26.

1. From these verses we see the purpose of the Lord's Table is "*in remembrance of me,*" the Lord Jesus Christ.

2. We also see how long we should do it, "*till He come.*"

3. We do not see how often we should do it. It just as "*as oft*" and "*as often.*"

This explains why different churches commemorate the Lord's death with different frequencies. I hope this helps.

> **1 Corinthians 11:24** *"And when he had given thanks, he brake it, and said, Take, eat: this is my body, which is broken for you: this do in remembrance of me."*
>
> **1 Corinthians 11:25** *"After the same manner also he took the cup, when he had supped, saying, This cup is the new testament in my blood: this do ye, as oft as ye drink it, in remembrance of me."*
>
> **1 Corinthians 11:26** *"For as often as ye eat this bread, and drink this cup, ye do shew the Lord's death till he come."*

Is Foot Washing An Ordinance?

QUESTION #1287

I wondered about rightly dividing the word of truth. Grace Brethren, for instance, go back to the Gospels to pick up foot washing as part of Communion, which I don't think is correct. Are there other situations where people go back to the Gospels and apply it incorrectly to the New Testament church? I know there are things in the Book of

Acts that should not be applied to the New Testament churches, but I wondered about foot washing in the Gospels.

ANSWER #1287

You're right about the Grace Brethren using foot washing taken from the Gospels. The Pentecostals and Charismatics also use the miracles and tongues in the Gospels and Acts to further their errors, though they all ceased when the Bible was completed for us in 90 or 100 A.D.

Another error that Dr. Thomas Strouse in Connecticut and others follow is that they put the beginning of the church in the Gospels, making Judas and the other eleven apostles members of this church. The announcement of the church in the future was made by the Lord Jesus Christ in Matthew, but the beginning of the church came with the descent of God the Holy Spirit in Acts 2. There are probably other errors that some teach today from the Gospels, but these are a few.

True Baptist Churches?

QUESTION #1288

One of our sons goes to a Baptist church that teaches that their Baptist church is a true New Testament church based upon Matthew 16:18, which says:

> "And I say also unto thee, That thou art Peter,
> and upon this rock I will build my church; and
> the gates of hell shall not prevail against it."

They say that other Baptist churches who disagree with them are not true Baptist churches. Are they correct?

ANSWER #1288

I know the young man who is the pastor of that church. He is a follower of Thomas Strouse in Connecticut. Strouse wrongly teaches that his brand of Baptists are the **only** body of Christ and other genuine Christians are only in the family of God. He misinterprets 1 Corinthians 12:13 and thinks the *"Spirit"* [God the Holy Spirit] should be only *"spirit"* [enthusiasm] with a small "s." He believes this is water baptism rather than Spirit baptism. He believes that only water baptism into his and similar Baptist churches makes a person a member of the *"body of Christ."* The truth is that all genuinely born-again and saved Christians (of whatever denomination or group they might attend) are members of *"the church which His body"* as clearly referred to in Ephesians 1:22-23.

> **Ephesians 1:22** *"And hath put all things
> under his feet, and gave him to be the head over
> all things to **the church**,"*

Ephesians 1:23 *"Which is his body, the fulness of him that filleth all in all."*

The Great Commission Applied
QUESTION #1289
I heard a Baptist pastor say that they were the true Baptist Church and that Jesus has only authorized them to do the Great Commission. They were the only ones who could administer communion and baptize people. Does this mean the Baptist Church I go to (as a born-again Christian) is not the true Baptist Church?
ANSWER #1289
Every sound church should seek to follow the Great Commission and send out the Bible's gospel of the Lord Jesus Christ. This sounds like a form of the heretical Landmark Baptist teaching. It sounds like this pastor believes in Baptist secessionism, so that if you're not in the "line," you're not a real Baptist. I believe our churches can use the name of Baptist (as our own Bible For Today Baptist Church does), and yet do not need to be connected with a succession of former Baptist churches from the first century onward. Each local Baptist church must be able to be independent and not joined tightly with any other entity, including some larger so-called "Baptist" movement.

Prayer To The Holy Spirit?
QUESTION #1290
There have been a couple songs that I'm wondering about that the church has used lately. The songs are being sung to the Holy Spirit. This is a deviation from the norm, as usually they use the old hymns. The following are some of the words to the song used today. Is it Biblical?

"Come Holy Spirit I need you
Come in thy strength and power
Come in thine own gentle way"
ANSWER #1290
It sounds like this church is slowly moving into "Contemporary Christian Music." The Bible never once tells us to pray to the Holy Spirit. This is unscriptural and unBiblical! The Lord Jesus Christ taught His disciples to pray to God the Father in His Name. Even in the disciples' prayer, He taught them to say *"Our Father."* I do not know any verse in the Bible, Old or New Testaments, which directs Christians to pray to God the Holy Spirit. This comes from Pentecostalism and the Charismatic movement.

Please see below.

> **John 15:16** *"Ye have not chosen me, but I have chosen you, and ordained you, that ye should go and bring forth fruit, and that your fruit should remain: that **whatsoever ye shall ask of the Father in my name, he may give it you**."*
>
> **John 16:23** *"And in that day ye shall ask me nothing. Verily, verily, I say unto you, **Whatsoever ye shall ask the Father in my name, he will give it you**."*
>
> **Matthew 6:9**   "**After this manner therefore pray ye: Our Father** which art in heaven, Hallowed be thy name."
>
> **Luke 11:2** "And he said unto them, **When ye pray, say, Our Father** which art in heaven, Hallowed be thy name. Thy kingdom come. Thy will be done, as in heaven, so in earth."

Are House Churches Biblical?
QUESTION #1291
Although I like many of David Cloud's books and articles, I'm disappointed that this book doesn't appear to talk about the "positives" of a *"house church,"* especially in these times of apostasy. We live in Texas and what used to be called the "Bible belt." But finding a "sound" church without ecumenicalism and apostasy is like finding a needle in a haystack! We are very thankful to God for bringing us to the Bible For Today Baptist Church in your home. How would you answer David Cloud's criticisms of *"house churches"*?

ANSWER #1291
It seems as though he despises house churches and agrees that a person should go to a church that is not really sound and separated just so he can go into a large building. Examples of Christians who met in houses are found in the New Testament. Nothing at all is said against this practice. Here is a list of 10 house churches in the New Testament that met in houses.

10 New Testament Church Groups That Met In Houses
1.   Acts 2:2
[2] And suddenly there came a sound from heaven as of a rushing mighty wind, and **it filled all the house where they were sitting**. (KJV)

2.   Acts 2:46

[46] And they, continuing daily with one accord in the temple, and **breaking bread from house to house**, did eat their meat with gladness and singleness of heart, (KJV)

3.   Acts 5:42

[42] And daily **in the temple, and in every house, they ceased not to teach and preach Jesus Christ**. (KJV)

4.   Acts 12:12

[12] And when he had considered *the thing*, **he came to the house of Mary the mother of John, whose surname was Mark; where many were gathered together praying**. (KJV)

5.   Acts 20:20

[20] *And* how I kept back nothing that was profitable *unto you*, but have shewed you, and **have taught you publickly, and from house to house**, (KJV)

6.   Acts 28:30

[30] And **Paul dwelt two whole years in his own hired house, and received all that came in unto him**, (KJV)

7.   Romans 16:5

[5] Likewise ***greet* the church that is in their house**. Salute my wellbeloved Epaenetus, who is the firstfruits of Achaia unto Christ. (KJV)

8.   1 Corinthians 16:19

[19] **The churches of Asia salute you. Aquila and Priscilla salute you much in the Lord, with the church that is in their house**. (KJV)

9.   Colossians 4:15

[15] Salute the brethren which are in Laodicea, and Nymphas, **and the church which is in his house**. (KJV)

10.   Philemon 2

[2] And to *our* beloved Apphia, and Archippus our fellowsoldier, **and to the church in thy house**: (KJV)

The Internet And Church Services
QUESTION #1292

http://www.theblaze.com/stories/2015/02/18/the-worship-trend-that-nearly-half-of-pastors-believe-could-be-possible-for-some-christians-in-the-next-decade/

Do people know how the Internet has made more people around the world able to hear sound Church services? The above LINK shows this.

ANSWER #1292

Thanks for this article. It indicates a large swelling of the use of the Internet for church services. However, finding sound and Biblical church services on the Internet is not so easy as time goes on. The apostates, the cults, the emerging church groups, the charismatics, the compromised new evangelicals, and all the other non-Biblical groups will also be out there seeking to draw in people for their attention and their funds. I'm glad that all of the services and ministries of our Bible For Today Baptist Church can be seen and heard 24 hours a day, 7 days a week, 356 days a year by going to our LINK: BibleForToday.org.

Though there are many LINKS on the first page, the **BROWN BOX** is where the verse-by-verse streaming-preaching and teaching morning services are found. I go from Romans through Revelation on a 16-week cycle. I take a half chapter each service, explaining each verse and using many other verses on similar topics.

The **YELLOW BOX** enables people to see current services by clicking on Sunday a.m. services, Sunday p.m. services, or Thursday p.m. services.

Women Preachers

QUESTION #1293

Is it all right for a woman to be a street-preacher or to be a pastor in a church?

ANSWER #1293

No, it is not Biblical for a woman either to do "street-preaching" or to be a "pastor" in any way, whether in a church, or on the street. A woman can witness about the Lord Jesus Christ to people on a one-to-one basis, but not "*preach*" to a church or a crowd of people and assume the role of a "pastor" or "bishop" or "elder" (three titles for the same office) whose qualifications in the Bible are clear as the following verses show and are limited to men only.

> **1 Timothy 3:2** "*A bishop then must be blameless, the **husband of one wife**, vigilant, sober, of good behaviour, given to hospitality, apt to teach;*"

> **Titus 1:5** "*For this cause left I thee in Crete, that thou shouldest set in order the things that are wanting, and ordain elders in every city, as I had appointed thee:*"

Titus 1:6   *"If any be blameless, **the husband of one wife**, having faithful children not accused of riot or unruly."*

Separation From False Brethren
QUESTION #1294

2 Thessalonians 3:6 *"Now we command you, brethren, in the name of our Lord Jesus Christ, that ye **withdraw yourselves from every brother that walketh disorderly, and not after the tradition which he received of us**."*

Does the verse above mean that if someone had relatives and they drank wine at family dinners, such as Thanksgiving, that genuine Christians should not go to that family dinner? Also, what does a Christian wife do whose husband is a Christian and drinks alcohol at times?

ANSWER #1294

I believe this verse refers to what some call "secondary separation." The problem is how you define "*disorderly*." I think the primary understanding of it is those who profess to be "brothers" (that is, true Christians), and yet they think nothing is wrong with other Christians who continue fellowship with apostate unbelievers such as in the National Council of Churches or other apostate groups. Obedient Christians should not have close fellowship with such Christians.

I believe in a secondary sense of what "*disorderly*" is might refer to alleged Christians who take alcohol or other drugs and think nothing of it. Or those who are living in adultery. Or those who are living in fornication. Or those who are homosexuals of either male or female. Or those homosexuals who are married to each other. Or a number of other immoral activities. They are indeed walking "*disorderly*."

When it comes to marriage and the relation between a Christian wife, and her Christian husband who might drink alcohol or where those at family dinners drink alcohol, it is more difficult to separate from these situations. Very, very strictly interpreted, the case could be made for separation. More loosely interpreted, since family is involved, the case could be made not to separate. One thing is for sure--genuine Christians should never participate in any disorderly activities. If the temptation is too great or might be too great, they should not even go where these disorderly activities are taking place.

2 Thessalonians 3:6 *"Now we command you, brethren, in the name of our Lord Jesus Christ, that ye withdraw yourselves from every brother that walketh disorderly, and not after the tradition which he received of us."*

Bible Separation
QUESTION #1295

Would you explain the Scriptures to me on this situation so I can help someone else understand that a person is not to stay in a church that is falling into apostasy and try to change it but is to just go and find another church.

ANSWER #1295

The verses below are the New Testament major verses on Biblical Separation From Apostates and Apostasy. God commands genuine Christians to stop being unequally yoked together with unbelievers. I have numbered the five questions God asks giving the reasons for separating from these unbelievers. And the final command of verse 17 is very clear, "*come out from among them, and be ye separate, saith the Lord, and touch not the unclean thing.*"

But remember this. Just because the Bible is crystal clear about this subject of separating from apostasy, it doesn't mean that those who are involved with it will indeed separate from it and come out from it. Don't hold your breath! Some obey the Bible, but many do not when it comes to this subject.

2 Corinthians 6:14 *"Be ye not unequally yoked together with unbelievers: (1) for what fellowship hath righteousness with unrighteousness? (2) and what communion hath light with darkness?"*

2 Corinthians 6:15 *"(3) And what concord hath Christ with Belial? or (4) what part hath he that believeth with an infidel?"*

2 Corinthians 6:16 *"(5) And what agreement hath the temple of God with idols? for ye are the temple of the living God; as God hath said, I will dwell in them, and walk in them; and I will be their God, and they shall be my people."*

2 Corinthians 6:17 *"**Wherefore come out from among them, and be ye separate, saith the Lord, and touch not the unclean thing; and I will receive you,**"*

2 Corinthians 6:18 *"And will be a Father unto you, and ye shall be my sons and daughters, saith the Lord Almighty."*

Bible Separation #2

QUESTION #1296

I need to know how to explain the Scriptures of separating from a church that has gone into more apostasy and that a person is to separate from that church. I know of a person who thinks that she should stay in a church falling into more apostasy. I told her that she is not to stay in it, but just leave it. How can I explain the Scriptures so she understands not to stay in the church but to leave it?

ANSWER #1296

Let me just say a few additional things about the important subject of Biblical separation:

1.   The verses of 2 Corinthians 6:14 and following clearly command obedient Christians to separate from the "unequal yoke" with "unbelievers." If apostasy is within this church in false doctrine from the pulpit or false doctrine in the doctrinal statements, it is an *"unequal yoke"* and the person is **commanded** to *"come out from them"* and *"be separate"* from them *"touch not the unclean thing."*

2.   How does this person know that they will be able, single-handedly, to either prevent the church from going into more apostasy, or even get rid of the apostasy already there? This would take many, many important leaders of that church to oust the apostates, then change the apostate doctrines to Biblical ones. Where are they going to get these many, many leaders who wish to do this?

3.   Furthermore, history has told us that there has never been a church or a group that has gone into apostasy that has ever rooted out that apostasy and brought 100% of sound, Biblical doctrines back into the church or group. It has never happened in the past history of the church, it will never happen in these days, and it will never happen in the future, if history is any indication of what does and does not happen.

4.   I would just quit talking with these people who think they can throw out the apostasy and the apostates and bring the church back to pure Bible truth. They are seeking to perform a fruitless, hopeless, and impossible task, and, if they turn a deaf ear to the Bible's truth on this subject, you are wasting your time trying to convince them otherwise.

Contemporary Christian Music (CCM)

QUESTION #1297

If a church uses Contemporary Christian Music (CCM) and worldly materials for Vacation Bible School, should people separate from such a church?

ANSWER #1297

The verse below commands the genuine Christians in the church at Philippi to "*think on these things.*" I have numbered 8 of them below. It would seem like CCM, the worldly VBS, and the worldly things in the church would not meet #4 of being "*pure.*"

The second set of verses from 1 John 2:15-17 command true Christians to "*love not the world.*" All CCM facilitates pride and lust. CCM's moods, rhythms, and words open the viewer and listener to entertainment at the expense of worship. Likewise, worldly VBS programs steer the students to less godliness and more simple entertainment.

Again, no matter how much you discuss or talk with this person about this, if they are determined to stay in the church because of their many friends, and associates, and many other reasons, they will not leave this church. If this is the case, in my considered opinion, it is a waste of your time to try to convince them otherwise.

Philippians 4:8 "*Finally, brethren,(1) whatsoever things are true, (2) whatsoever things are honest, (3) whatsoever things are just, (4) whatsoever things are pure, (5) whatsoever things are lovely, (6) whatsoever things are of good report; (7) if there be any virtue, and (8) if there be any praise, think on these things.*"

1 John 2:15 "*Love not the world, neither the things that are in the world. If any man love the world, the love of the Father is not in him.*"

1 John 2:16 "*For all that is in the world, the lust of the flesh, and the lust of the eyes, and the pride of life, is not of the Father, but is of the world.*"

1 John 2:17 "*And the world passeth away, and the lust thereof: but he that doeth the will of God abideth for ever.*"

Internet Church Ministries #2

QUESTION #1298

You mentioned about how some people think an online church does not count like being there in person. Is an online church Biblical in our days? I have chronic vertigo and am very limited in my driving. I have searched for a very long time, for a Bible-teaching church, and have been very blessed by your teachings, and Pastor Daniel's teachings. Thank you for offering your services and Bible studies in real time.

ANSWER #1298

I firmly believe that an online church is Biblical in our days. Thank you for your encouraging remarks in defense of our Internet preaching, Bible studies, and Pastor Daniel's important classes each week. I am sorry for your chronic vertigo, but I am very glad that Pastor Daniel's expertise has made our church able to send out our services to friends like you so that you can be blessed by the Lord Jesus Christ by feasting on His precious Words.

CHAPTER VIII
QUESTIONS ABOUT
VARIOUS MORAL QUESTIONS

Marriages With Relatives
QUESTION #1299

One of my neighbors came to see me about a sinful relationship between their ex-spouse and a cousin of their ex's. My neighbor's ex belongs to the Jehovah Witness religious cult. My neighbor's father-in-law does not discourage or disagree with this illicit liaison, because the father-in-law says the Bible does not speak against it. Any information you are able to share will certainly be greatly appreciated and shall be a tremendous blessing to me, my neighbor, and all of the concerned family members.

ANSWER #1299

I assume your neighbor's ex-husband is committing adultery or fornication and having sexual relations with a cousin. I assume that he will either marry his cousin or just keep having sexual relations with her. I have two parts to my answer as to how the Bible speaks against these sins:

1.   **The Bible is clear about the sin of sexual relations with someone a person is not married to.**

Hebrews 13:4
"Marriage is honourable in all, and the bed undefiled: but whoremongers and adulterers God will judge."

Exodus 20:14 *"Thou shalt not commit adultery."*

Leviticus 20:10 *"And the man that committeth adultery with another man's wife, even he that committeth adultery with his neighbour's wife, the adulterer and the adulteress shall surely be put to death."*

Deuteronomy 5:18
"Neither shalt thou commit adultery."

Proverbs 6:32
"But whoso committeth adultery with a woman lacketh understanding: he that doeth it destroyeth his own soul."

Romans 1:29
"Being filled with all unrighteousness, fornication, wickedness, covetousness, maliciousness; full of envy, murder, debate, deceit, malignity; whisperers,"

1 Corinthians 6:13
"Meats for the belly, and the belly for meats: but God shall destroy both it and them. Now the body is not for fornication, but for the Lord; and the Lord for the body."

1 Corinthians 6:18
"Flee fornication. Every sin that a man doeth is without the body; but he that committeth fornication sinneth against his own body."

1 Corinthians 7:2
"Nevertheless, to avoid fornication, let every man have his own wife, and let every woman have her own husband."

Galatians 5:19
"Now the works of the flesh are manifest, which are these; Adultery, fornication, uncleanness, lasciviousness,"

Ephesians 5:3
"But fornication, and all uncleanness, or covetousness, let it not be once named among you, as becometh saints;"

Colossians 3:5
"Mortify therefore your members which are upon the earth; fornication, uncleanness, inordinate affection, evil concupiscence, and covetousness, which is idolatry:"

2.   **The Old Testament commands against marrying or having sexual relations with close relatives.**

[NOTE: In these verses, the expression "*uncover the nakedness*" refers to making a marriage with someone or having sexual relations with them.]

Leviticus 18:12

"Thou shalt not uncover the nakedness of thy father's sister: she is thy father's near kinswoman."

Leviticus 18:13

"Thou shalt not uncover the nakedness of thy mother's sister: for she is thy mother's near kinswoman."

Leviticus 18:14

"Thou shalt not uncover the nakedness of thy father's brother, thou shalt not approach to his wife: she is thine aunt."

Leviticus 18:15

"Thou shalt not uncover the nakedness of thy daughter in law: she is thy son's wife; thou shalt not uncover her nakedness."

Leviticus 18:16

"Thou shalt not uncover the nakedness of thy brother's wife: it is thy brother's nakedness."

Leviticus 18:17

"Thou shalt not uncover the nakedness of a woman and her daughter, neither shalt thou take her son's daughter, or her daughter's daughter, to uncover her nakedness; for they are her near kinswomen: it is wickedness."

Leviticus 20:19

"And thou shalt not uncover the nakedness of thy mother's sister, nor of thy father's sister: for he uncovereth his near kin: they shall bear their iniquity."

I hope this gives you and your neighbors a Biblical basis in order to assess their sinful behaviors.

Miscegenation Marriages
QUESTION #1300

Have you ever preached or taught on miscegenation?

ANSWER #1300

No, I have not, but the Old Testament is very clear that in the line of Shem, the Semites were never to intermarry with and have children by the line of Ham. Ham means *"black," "dark,"* or *"dusky."* All the Canaanite tribes listed in Genesis 10 were Hamites. Ezra and Nehemiah had trouble with the returning Jews after 70 years in

Babylon with the Jews intermarrying and having children with the Canaanite races of Ham. They broke up these marriages.

Though the New Testament is not precise on this, nature itself teaches us that when there is a choice, dogs breed with their own kind, and birds with their own kind, as well as other creatures. There is not always a choice, so there is interbreeding among these and other animals. Of course TV and Hollywood have been pushing interracial marriages and children quite strongly. The ones I have special concern for is their children. They don't know if they are White or Black, and many times they have blotches on their skin.

The Meaning of "Fornication"
QUESTION #1301
Do we include all sorts of immoral sexual behavior under the term fornication, porneia?   Is adultery considered a form of fornication?

ANSWER #1301
In our legal system, I believe fornication is sexual relations between unmarried people and adultery is sexual relations by one who is married.

The Greek term, PORNEIA, however, as mentioned below includes many different kinds of sexual behaviors.

> PORNEIA (he-): n.fem.; "fornication, sexual immorality, sexual sin of a general kind, that includes many different behaviors (Mt 5:32; 15:19; 19:9; Mk 7:21; Jn 8:41; Ac 15:20; 1Co 6:18; 7:2; 2Co 12:21; Gal 5:19; Eph 5:3; 1Th 4:3)

The Meaning of "Fornication" #2
QUESTION #1302
What is the distinction between "fornication," "adultery," and other "sexual sins" mentioned in some Bible versions?

ANSWER #1302
The LINK below gives many illustrations and definitions of these various terms as well as "sexual immorality" and other general phrases that have been used by other Bible versions. This is a very helpful and detailed article on this important subject.
http://www.rmsbibleengineering.com/Page2/Adultery/Page2_1.html

Nakedness And Modest Dress

QUESTION #1303

Does God specify what nakedness or what modest dress is? How would I explain this to someone?

ANSWER #1303

The word "*naked*" or "*nakedness*" occurs 87 times in our King James Bible. Depending on the context, it means that there is very little covering, if any. When Peter jumped into the water in the verse below, the Greek word used for "*naked*" was GUMNOS. We get the word gym and gymnasium from it. It meant that Peter did not have his outer clothing on which he normally wore, but just his underclothing on while in the boat. Just like those in the gym have fewer clothes than when out on the street, so "*naked*" often has that meaning.

At times, it means literally without any clothes or covering of any kind.

As for modest dress for women it would seem, as a minimum, loose-fitting clothing on the top and on the bottom of it (like a loose skirt or dress) which at least covers the knees and also is no more than two or three inches from the neck to cover the breasts. That would be my answer to your question.

> **1 Timothy 2:9** "*In like manner also, that women adorn themselves in modest apparel, with shamefacedness and sobriety; not with broided hair, or gold, or pearls, or costly array;*"

The Greek word for "***modest***" in the verse below, is KOSMIOS. Some of the meanings for this Greek Word are:

> "*pertaining to being modest in the sense of moderate and well-ordered—'modest, well-ordered, moderate, becoming.' 'the church leader must be sober, self-controlled, moderate 1 Tm. 3:2; in modest apparel' 1 Tm 2:9. For another interpretation of in 1 Tm 2:9, see 66.10. 8.49 f: the quality of modesty, with the implication of resulting respect—'modesty.' 'that women dress themselves in becoming clothing, modestly, and properly' 1 Tm 2:9.*

> **John 21:7** "*Therefore that disciple whom Jesus loved saith unto Peter, It is the Lord. Now when Simon Peter heard that it was the Lord, he girt his fisher's coat unto him, (for he was **naked**,) and did cast himself into the sea.*"

1 Timothy 2:9 *"In like manner also, that women adorn themselves in __modest apparel__, with shamefacedness and sobriety; not with broided hair, or gold, or pearls, or costly array;"*

Noah's Nakedness In His Tent
QUESTION #1304

Do you think that Noah's wife may have been in that tent when Noah was passed out, and when Ham came in? I know that there is no indication of this in the Bible. What do you think happened here? I find this is a controversy that has gone on a long time and has many theories.

ANSWER #1304

From the verses below, Ham (apparently the youngest son of Noah), saw the nakedness of his father. Shem and Japheth covered their father's nakedness but they did not see Noah's nakedness. When Noah awoke from his drunken stupor, he saw what Ham *"had done unto him."* There is no homosexual relationship mentioned here. I believe the sin of Ham was going into his father's tent at all. That's what was *"done"* unto Noah.

I suppose Canaan was made a servant of both Shem and of Japheth probably because he was young and able to serve these brothers whereas Ham might have been old and feeble and unable to serve. I think we should be very careful about following conclusions that are not clearly in the Bible.

Genesis 9:20 *"And Noah began to be an husbandman, and he planted a vineyard:"*

Genesis 9:21 *"And he drank of the wine, and was drunken; and he was uncovered within his tent."*

Genesis 9:22 *"And Ham, the father of Canaan, saw the nakedness of his father, and told his two brethren without."*

Genesis 9:23 *"And Shem and Japheth took a garment, and laid it upon both their shoulders, and went backward, and covered the nakedness of their father; and their faces were backward, and they saw not their father's nakedness."*

Genesis 9:24 *"And Noah awoke from his wine, and knew what his younger son had done unto him."*

Genesis 9:25 *"And he said, Cursed be Canaan; a servant of servants shall he be unto his brethren."*

Genesis 9:26 *"And he said, Blessed be the LORD God of Shem; and Canaan shall be his servant."*

Genesis 9:27 *"God shall enlarge Japheth, and he shall dwell in the tents of Shem; and Canaan shall be his servant."*

Eunuchs vs. Homosexuals

QUESTION #1305

Is *"eunuch"* used interchangeably for *"homosexuals"* in the Bible? I can't trust the Internet for an honest answer.

ANSWER #1305

The word "eunuch" occurs 23 times in our King James Bible. In every instance it refers to a male who has been castrated. It never refers to a homosexual. The expanded definition is below.

"(sa-rîs) official, eunuch. (ASV, RSV similarly.) The noun, meaning "(court) official," has its origin in the Akkadian title ša re?ši (šarri) "the one of the (king's) head." The meaning "eunuch" arose with the practice of utilizing castrated men in key positions in the various nations of the ancient near east (e.g. in Persia, Est 2:3ff.; 4:4f.).

"The Hebrew word is clearly related to the name of the Akkadian royal official (II Kings 18:17). Accordingly, sa-rîs is not to be translated "eunuch" unless context or other evidence demands it. Thus, since thorough study fails to uncover conclusive evidence for the employment of eunuchs as officials in ancient Egypt, the reason why the Egyptian officers in the Joseph narrative were called by this term is probably that in all three cases (Gen 37:36; 39:1; 40:2, 7) these men were special officials of Pharaoh."

"It can be doubted that Israel would have inaugurated the employment of eunuchs. Such men would have been excluded from the congregation by Mosaic Law (Lev 22:24; Deut 23:2). It has been argued that they may have been introduced by Jezebel (cf. I Kings 22:9) and

maintained by subsequent kings (*II Kings 8:6; 9:32*) in positions in close contact with women. If so, the Lord's promise through Isaiah (*56:3–5*) is most apropos. No certain evidence exists that Daniel and his three friends were made eunuchs (*II Kings 20:17–18; Dan 1*). Bibliography: *TDNT*, II, pp. 766–67. R. D. Patterson, In Theological Wordbook of the Old Testament, ed. R. Laird Harris, Gleason L. Archer, Jr. and Bruce K. Waltke, electronic ed. (Chicago: Moody Press, 1999), 634-35.*"*

The Salem Witch Trial
QUESTION #1306
Do you have any information on the Salem witch trial in the American colonies?
ANSWER #1306
The LINK below seems to sum up most of these trials.
http://en.wikipedia.org/wiki/Salem_witch_trials

Should We Marry Homosexuals?
QUESTION #1307
Should I as a pastor marry homosexual couples?
ANSWER #1307
Even though a recent article came out which states that an Idaho pastor should perform same-sex weddings or face jail, Acts 5:29 is very clear that genuine Christians, including pastors, should obey God rather than men, despite the consequences!

> **Acts 5:29** *"Then Peter and the other apostles answered and said, We ought to obey God rather than men."* (Acts 5:29)

The Knapps now face a 180-day jail term and $1,000 fine for each day they decline to celebrate the same-sex wedding.

> **2 Timothy 3:1** *"This know also, that in the last days perilous times shall come."* (2 Timothy 3:1)

Homosexuality is clearly condemned both in the Old Testament and in the New Testament.

> **Leviticus 18:22** *"Thou shalt not lie with mankind, as with womankind: it is abomination."*

> **Leviticus 20:13** *"If a man also lie with mankind, as he lieth with a woman, both of them have committed an abomination: they shall surely be put to death; their blood shall be upon them."*
>
> **Romans 1:26** *"For this cause God gave them up unto vile affections: for even their women did change the natural use into that which is against nature:"*
>
> **Romans 1:27** *"And likewise also the men, leaving the natural use of the woman, burned in their lust one toward another; men with men working that which is unseemly, and receiving in themselves that recompence of their error which was meet."*

Since Obama took office January 20, 2009, dozens of laws and executive orders have been quietly put in place to create an environment that is heavily in favor of LGBT policies and practices; these have nothing to do with *"tolerance"* or *"acceptance of diversity,"* but rather seek to silence and instill fear in any and all who would oppose their radical agenda. Christianity and the Bible are under direct attack in America, and we are about to live to see the day where preachers of the old-fashioned gospel who preach against the sin of homosexuality will watch as their churches are taken from them, and they themselves are placed in jail.

Marriage Is To Be Permanent
QUESTION #1308

Someone discussed remarriage in 1 Corinthians 7:27-28. He explained that these verses refer to a person who remarried another spouse after a divorce had taken place. He said then he had not sinned. Is this Biblical?

> **1 Corinthians 7:27-28** *"<u>Art thou bound unto a wife? seek not to be loosed. Art thou loosed from a wife? seek not a wife</u>. But and if thou marry, thou hast not sinned; and if a virgin marry, she hath not sinned. Nevertheless such shall have trouble in the flesh: but I spare you."*

ANSWER #1308

I do not agree with the person you are quoting. The verses are clear, *"Art thou loosed from a wife? Seek not a wife."* Verse 27 is very clear. These people are not to re-marry while their mate is still living.

Verse 28, however, refers to people who have never been married at all. It is all right for them to marry. A virgin who has never been married can be married. This does not violate any Biblical doctrine. Both of the cases in verse 28 refer to first marriages. They are not re-marriages.

Divorce And Remarriage
QUESTION #1309

I so appreciate your synopsis of Brother Sorenson's commentary. May I ask what your position is on divorce and remarriage? This has been an issue that I have been struggling with for a few years.

ANSWER #1309

I differ strongly with Sorenson's views on divorce and remarriage. I believe they're unscriptural. My position on divorce and remarriage is found in the verses below. They clearly teach that only death breaks the marriage bond. That is my position. Sorenson wrongly teaches that something other than death can break marriage. He teaches that a person is free to re-marry even while the mate is still alive. I believe that is a totally unscriptural position.

He, and many others, misinterpret the verses below in Matthew which describe the Jewish practice of betrothal—not marriage. It was similar to marriage, but the parties did not come together sexually. That state of betrothal could be broken if there was fornication on the part of either mate. This was "divorce" that was permitted from betrothal. It was not divorce from a valid actual full-blown "marriage" after it had been consummated. See the references below for Mark and Luke. These verses explain what the Bible clearly teaches on this subject. I agree with the Bible on this and disagree with Sorenson and all others who agree with his unscriptural position.

> **Matthew 5:32** *"But I say unto you, That whosoever shall put away his wife, saving for the cause of fornication, causeth her to commit adultery: and whosoever shall marry her that is divorced committeth adultery."*

Being in the Gospel of Matthew, who is writing to the Jews especially, this refers to their Jewish custom of betrothal, not to an actual and legitimate marriage.

> **Matthew 19:9** *"And I say unto you, Whosoever shall put away his wife, except it be for fornication, and shall marry another, committeth adultery: and whoso marrieth her which is put away doth commit adultery."*

Once again, being in the Gospel of Matthew, which was written to the Jews especially, this refers to their Jewish custom of betrothal, not to an actual and legitimate marriage.

Mark and Luke are clear in this matter. Neither of them is writing specifically to the Jews. They do not speak of the Jewish custom of betrothal, but of actual and legitimate marriage.

Mark 10:11 *"And he saith unto them, Whosoever shall put away his wife, and marry another, committeth adultery against her."*

Mark 10:12 *"And if a woman shall put away her husband, and be married to another, she committeth adultery."*

Luke 16:18 *"Whosoever putteth away his wife, and marrieth another, committeth adultery: and whosoever marrieth her that is put away from her husband committeth adultery."*

Paul is clear on this subject as well, both in 1 Corinthians 7 and in Romans 7.

1 Corinthians 7:10   *"And unto the married I command, yet not I, but the Lord, Let not the wife depart from her husband:"*

1 Corinthians 7:11 *"But and if she depart, let her remain unmarried, or be reconciled to her husband: and let not the husband put away his wife."*

Romans 7:2 *"For the woman which hath an husband is bound by the law to her husband so long as he liveth; but if the husband be dead, she is loosed from the law of her husband."*

Romans 7:3 *"So then if, while her husband liveth, she be married to another man, she shall be called an adulteress: but if her husband be dead, she is free from that law; so that she is no adulteress, though she be married to another man."*

Many Wives
QUESTION #1310

In the Old Testament men had many wives. Why was this instead of one man and one wife only?

ANSWER #1310

God's original will in the Garden of Eden was for marriage to be between one man and one woman until the death of the mate. During the dispensation of Conscience, bigamy began with Lamech who took two wives.

> **Genesis 4:19** *"And **Lamech took unto him two wives**: the name of the one was Adah, and the name of the other Zillah."*)

Then in the dispensation of Promise, there were more extra wives. In the dispensation of the Law, many wives occurred again including Solomon's 1,001 women. These multi-marriages were not God's will for people.

The New Testament is very clear on this subject, though many, (even some genuine Christians) disregard His standards. Marriage is to be as long as the mate is living. To re-marry while the mate is still living is to commit adultery against the living mate.

> **Mark 10:11** *"And he saith unto them, **Whosoever shall put away his wife, and marry another, committeth adultery against her**."*

> **Luke 16:18** *"**Whosoever putteth away his wife, and marrieth another, committeth adultery: and whosoever marrieth her that is put away from her husband committeth adultery**."*

> **Romans 7:2** *"For **the woman which hath an husband is bound by the law to her husband so long as he liveth**; but if the husband be dead, she is loosed from the law of her husband."*

> **Romans 7:3** *"**So then if, while her husband liveth, she be married to another man, she shall be called an adulteress**: but if her husband be dead, she is free from that law; so that she is no adulteress, though she be married to another man."*

> **1 Corinthians 7:39** **The wife is bound by the law as long as her husband liveth**; but if her husband be dead, she is at liberty to be married to whom she will; only in the Lord.

Jonathan And David's Relationship
QUESTION #1311
What was the relationship between Saul's son, Jonathan, and David? The pro-gay commentators have been doing a considerable amount of "reading into" the verses on this subject, calling it a homosexual relationship. What is the answer?

ANSWER #1311
I think there was a strong respect and faith that both men had in the Lord. They were valiant and faithful to the Lord. This was an admiring love that David had for Jonathan. David had many wives. He was not a homosexual, nor are these verses listed below to be interpreted the way the homosexuals interpret them today, trying to evidence homosexuality on both David's and Jonathan's parts.

> **1 Samuel 18:1** *"And it came to pass, when he had made an end of speaking unto Saul, that the soul of Jonathan was knit with the soul of David, and **Jonathan loved him as his own soul**."*

> **1 Samuel 18:3** *"Then Jonathan and David made a covenant, because **he loved him as his own soul**."*

> **2 Samuel 1:26** *"I am distressed for thee, my brother Jonathan: very pleasant hast thou been unto me: **thy love to me was wonderful, passing the love of women**."*

Adultery
QUESTION #1312
Pastor, I noticed this week in our daily Bible reading God's commandment regarding adultery:

> **Deuteronomy 22:22-24**
> *22 If a man be found lying with a woman married to an husband, then they shall both of them die, both the man that lay with the woman, and the woman: so shalt thou put away evil from Israel.*
> *23 If a damsel that is a virgin be betrothed unto an husband, and a man find her in the city, and lie with her;*
> *24 **Then ye shall bring them both out unto the gate of that city, and ye shall stone them with stones** that they die; the damsel,*

because she cried not, being in the city; and the man, because he hath humbled his neighbour's wife: so thou shalt put away evil from among you.

John 8 King James Version

8:1 Jesus went unto the mount of Olives.

2 And early in the morning he came again into the temple, and all the people came unto him; and he sat down, and taught them.

3 And the scribes and Pharisees brought unto him a woman taken in adultery; and when they had set her in the midst,

*4 They say unto him, **Master, this woman was taken in adultery, in the very act.***

***5 Now Moses in the law commanded us, that such should be stoned: but what sayest thou**?*

6 This they said, tempting him, that they might have to accuse him. But Jesus stooped down, and with his finger wrote on the ground, as though he heard them not.

7 So when they continued asking him, he lifted up himself, and said unto them, He that is without sin among you, let him first cast a stone at her.

8 And again he stooped down, and wrote on the ground,

9 And they which heard it, being convicted by their own conscience, went out one by one, beginning at the eldest, even unto the last: and Jesus was left alone, and the woman standing in the midst.

10 When Jesus had lifted up himself, and saw none but the woman, he said unto her, Woman, where are those thine accusers? hath no man condemned thee?

11 She said, No man, Lord. And Jesus said unto her, Neither do I condemn thee: go, and sin no more.

Why weren't the men also to be stoned? They also committed adultery if they were married.

ANSWER #1312

You are right that the Pharisees wanted only the woman to be stoned, but not the man. That certainly was contrary to the Law of Moses. Even today, people add, subtract, and change God's Words regarding the Biblical sin of adultery.

CHAPTER IX
QUESTIONS ABOUT
MEANINGS OF VARIOUS TERMS

Greek Word, AION, As "Eternal"
QUESTION #1313
Why is the Greek word, AION, translated as "*eternal*" or "*everlasting*"?

ANSWER #1313
AION or AIONIOS literally means "AGE." Eternal or everlasting is "*ages upon ages*" or "*eternal.*" This is the sense and why AION sometimes means "*age*" or "*period of time,*" and sometimes means "*the ages of ages*" or "*eternal*" and "*everlasting.*"

Some of the meanings of AION given in a Greek lexicon are:
1. *eternal, an unlimited duration (Ro 16:26; Mk 16: Shorter v.r.); 2. since all time, time (long ago), (Ro 16:25)*

The Temptation Of Christ
QUESTION #1314
I have a question about Hebrews 4:15.

Hebrews 4:15 *"For we have not an high priest which cannot be touched with the feeling of our infirmities; but __was in all points tempted like as we are, yet without sin__."*

My question is: Does this mean that Jesus had infirmities or just could sympathize with our infirmities?

ANSWER #1314
The Lord Jesus Christ was tempted or tested as humans are because He was Perfect Man. He did not have any infirmities, but was sinless. Having seen the various infirmities of many of the people, and being Perfect Man because of his Incarnation by means of His virgin birth, the Lord Jesus Christ could sympathize with their infirmities though not having any of His own. In summary: because of His incarnation, and thus becoming perfect God and perfect Man, he could sympathize with every human being.

Flesh And Spirit Battles
QUESTION #1315

Romans 7:15   *"For **that which I do I allow not**: for what I would, that do I not; but what I hate, that do I."*

I am having trouble breaking down Romans 7:15 to understand it better. Could you give me a hand with it, please?

ANSWER #1315

I believe this verse illustrates the battle Paul was having, and all born-again genuine Christians have.   It is a battle between the person's flesh and the Holy Spirit Who indwells within them. When Paul said *"that which I do,"* he was speaking of what he was doing in the flesh, even though he didn't allow for it as being the leading of the Holy Spirit. But what Paul really wanted to do as guided by the Holy Spirit (*"what I would"*) he doesn't do because of the victory of his flesh (*"that do I not"*). What he hates (*"what I hate"*) and knows it is against the Bible, because of the power of his flesh, he does because he is walking after his flesh (*"that do I"*).

The following verses in Galatians 5 are comments on this battle between the flesh and the Holy Spirit within every genuine Christian.

Galatians 5:16   *"This I say then, Walk in the Spirit, and ye shall not fulfil the lust of the flesh."*

Galatians 5:17   *"For the flesh lusteth against the Spirit, and the Spirit against the flesh: and these are contrary the one to the other: so that ye cannot do the things that ye would."*

Righteousness In Christians
QUESTION #1316

I've been studying Romans 8:4, but finding it hard to get the answer. Is the following verse talking about the Christian?

Romans 8:4 *"**That the righteousness of the law might be fulfilled in us**, who walk not after the flesh, but after the Spirit."*

ANSWER #1316

Romans 8:1 *"**There is therefore now no condemnation to them which are in Christ Jesus**, who walk not after the flesh, but after the Spirit."*

Romans 8:2 *"For the law of the Spirit of life in Christ Jesus hath made me free from the law of sin and death."*

Romans 8:3 *"For what the law could not do, in that it was weak through the flesh, God sending his own Son in the likeness of sinful flesh, and for sin, condemned sin in the flesh:"*

Romans 8:4 *"That **the righteousness of the law might be fulfilled in us**, who walk not after the flesh, but after the Spirit."*

This verse declares that God considers *"the righteousness of the law"* of Moses has been fulfilled in every genuine Christian who is *"in Christ."*

Meaning Of Greek "Delivered"

QUESTION #1317

1 Thessalonians 1:10 *"And to wait for his Son from heaven, whom he raised from the dead, even Jesus, which **delivered us from the wrath to come**."*

Please share with me your refutation concerning I Thessalonians 1:10 and the use of "delivered" instead of "delivers" or "delivereth."

ANSWER #1317

The King James Bible translators took this present tense of RUOMAI as one of the special uses of the present tense called the aoristic present. Though present tense, its actions are point-actions like the aorist and are thus rendered in the past. This is explained fully in Dana and Mantey's Intermediate Greek Grammar, pages 184-185

I believe this deliverance from the *"wrath to come"* includes not only the fires of Hell, but also the going into any part of the seven-year Tribulation period.

Meaning Of 2 Chronicles 7:12-14

QUESTION #1318

2 Chronicles 7:12   *"And the LORD appeared to Solomon by night, and said unto him, I have heard thy prayer, and have chosen this place to myself for an house of sacrifice."*

2 Chronicles 7:13 *"If I shut up heaven that there be no rain, or if I command the locusts to devour the land, or if I send pestilence among my people;"*

> **2 Chronicles 7:14** *"If my people, which are called by my name, shall humble themselves, and pray, and seek my face, and turn from their wicked ways; then will I hear from heaven, and will forgive their sin, and will heal their land."*

The teaching was on 2 Chronicles 7:12-14. It seemed it was being applied to churches and what is going on in other countries where there is reported revival. The teaching was to get the church motivated for a tent revival. I would like your input on this.

ANSWER #1318

I believe that this passage was given directly to the nation of Israel and not to the church age at all. It has been wrongly applied to the age of grace and to the church on many occasions. Though there might be some general applications, these verses must be specifically applied to the nation of Israel rather than to the church.

1 John 5:6 Explained

QUESTION #1319

> **1 John 5:6** *"__This is he that came by water and blood, even Jesus Christ__; not by water only, but by water and blood. And it is the Spirit that beareth witness, because the Spirit is truth."*

I have been having a discussion on 1 John 5:6. How do you explain *"water and blood"* in this verse?

ANSWER #1319

In 1 John 3:5, I believe the *"water"* there might refer to the bag of water that breaks upon physical birth. To be born-again, we had to have a first birth and also a birth by God the Holy Spirit.

> **John 3:5** *"Jesus answered, Verily, verily, I say unto thee, __Except a man be born of water and of the Spirit__, he cannot enter into the kingdom of God."*

In 1 John 5:6, the water could possibly also refer to the fact that the Lord Jesus Christ was born physically from Mary. The "blood" could refer to the fact that the Lord Jesus Christ's blood came from God Himself through the miraculous virgin birth. His blood did not come from Adam as that of all mankind comes.

Acts 20:28 *"Take heed therefore unto yourselves, and to all the flock, over the which the Holy Ghost hath made you overseers, to feed the church of **God, which he hath purchased with his own blood**."*

The source of the blood of the Lord Jesus Christ was from God as Hebrews 10:5 indicates:

Hebrews 10:5   *"Wherefore when he cometh into the world, he saith, Sacrifice and offering thou wouldest not, but **a body hast thou prepared me**:"*

His "body" included every part, including His hair, bones, hands, blood, feet, brain and all other details.

Therefore, it is entirely possible that it was necessary for the Lord Jesus Christ to have a physical birth (water) but also had to have incorruptible and sinless blood which alone could atone for the sins of the world.

Jews And The Church
QUESTION #1320

Jews who are saved now--are they part of the church, or will they be part of the future earthly nation of Israel in the Kingdom?

ANSWER #1320

I believe that born-again Jews today are part of the church which is Christ's body (Ephesians 1:22-23. They are no longer considered Jews any more than we who were Gentiles. They, and we who are truly saved, are genuine Christians and members of the body of Christ.

I believe the Jews in the millennial reign of Christ in the kingdom, will be those who were the saints of the Old Testament and, perhaps, those who were converted by the preaching of the 144,000 Jewish evangelists during the Tribulation period. This is Daniel's 70th week, so it is part of the Old Testament legal period. So they would be part of the kingdom reign of Christ.

Meaning Of Galatians 6:16
QUESTION #1321

Galatians 6:16 *"And as many as walk according to this rule, peace be on them, and mercy, and upon **the Israel of God**."*

Does Galatians 6:16 refer to the Church or to "Ethnic" Israel?

ANSWER #1321

It is a difficult question, but from the context, it seems like the reference would be to godly Israel who, in Paul's day, had accepted Christ as Saviour and were therefore "godly." They would be part of the church which is His Body (Ephesians 1:22-23). Again, it's not clear, but that's what I would think about it.

The Meaning Of "Fountain"
QUESTION #1322

There are hymns like *"There is a Fountain Filled With Blood, Drawn From Emmanuel's Veins."* Where do they get the phrase in scripture about a *"Fountain"*? What is your opinion?

ANSWER #1322

There might be other explanations, but this idea possibly comes from the verse below. The atoning blood of the Lord Jesus Christ is the only thing that can forgive sin and uncleanness. Here it is called a fountain that looks forward from Zechariah's day to the cross of Calvary.

> Zechariah 13:1 *"**In that day there shall be a fountain opened to the house of David and to the inhabitants** of Jerusalem for sin and for uncleanness."*

The Meaning Of 2 Peter 3:12
QUESTION #1323

> 2 Peter 3:12 *"**Looking for** and **hasting** unto the coming of the day of God, wherein the heavens being on fire shall be dissolved, and the elements shall melt with fervent heat?"*

I have a question on 2 Peter 3:12. What does *"hasting"* actually mean there? We are looking for the Lord's coming, but how can we *"hasten"* or hurry to it?

ANSWER #1323

Of the various meanings of SPEUDO which is translated *"hasting,"* I think *"to be eager"* for the coming day of God would make the most sense. I think it goes along with *"looking for"* the best. *"Looking for"* meanings are also below:

> SPEUDO: *"1. do quickly, hasten, suddenness (Lk 2:16; 19:5, 6; Ac 20:16; 22:18+), for another interp, see last entry; 2. cause to happen soon (2Pe 3:12+); 3. 25.74 **be eager** (Ac*

20:16+), note: there may be overlap in the verses and entries"

PROSDOKAO *"1. wait with anxiety (Ac 27:33); 2. expect, look forward to the future (Mt 24:50)."*

The Meaning Of Romans 5:8

QUESTION #1324

Romans 5:8 *"But __God commendeth his love toward us__, in that, while we were yet sinners, Christ died for us."*

I am looking at Romans 5:8. What do the words mean: *"God commendeth his love toward us"*?

ANSWER #1324

The Greek Word for *"commendeth"* is SUNISTEMI. Of the various meanings, I think *"demonstrate"* is the best. God demonstrated His love toward us, in that, while we were yet sinners, Christ died for us.

SUNISTEMI 1. stand with (Lk 9:32+); 2. come into existence (2Pe 3:5+); 3. recommend, commend (Ro 16:1; 2Co 3:1; 4:2; 5:12; 10:12, 18; 12:11+); 4. **demonstrate** (Ro 3:5; 5:8; 2Co 6:4; 7:11; Gal 2:18+); 5. hold together in proper place or arrangement (Col 1:17+)"

The Meaning Of The Remnant

QUESTION #1325

The reason that *"remnant"* came up was a brochure I received in the mail. It is called, *"A Congress For The Christian Remnant-- The Remnant overcoming the world by Christ."* Doesn't the Bible use the *"remnant"* in referring to Israel?

ANSWER #1325

As I told you in my last note, of the 91 uses of *"remnant"* in the King James Bible, only 6 are found in the New Testament. Two of them might refer to the Christians today. I don't think we should ban the English word *"remnant"* altogether. There are *"remnants of cloth,"* etc.

It is logical also to use the word *"remnant"* today to refer to a very small group out of a larger group, just like the remnant of cloth is a very small part out of a larger part. In the Bible, the word *"remnant"* is almost exclusively referring to Israel; it is true in the days in which we live that the genuinely saved, born-again Christians are but a "*remnant*" of the billions of people around the globe. That is a perfectly good use of the word "remnant" in the current year outside the Biblical usage of the term. I think you should distinguish between the Bible's use and our use of it today referring to many other things.

Meaning Of 2 Corinthians 12:2-4
QUESTION #1326

2 Corinthians 12:2 *"I knew a man in Christ above fourteen years ago, (whether in the body, I cannot tell; or whether out of the body, I cannot tell: God knoweth;) **such an one caught up to the third heaven**."*

2 Corinthians 12:3 *"And I knew such a man, (whether in the body, or out of the body, I cannot tell: God knoweth;)"*

2 Corinthians 12:4 *"How that he was caught up into paradise, and heard unspeakable words, which it is not lawful for a man to utter."*

I have a question on 2 Corinthian 12:2-4. There is a mention of the 3rd heaven. What does this mean?

ANSWER #1326

I believe Paul is commenting on what happened in Acts 14:19 (about 14 years before 2 Corinthians).

Acts 14:18 *"And with these sayings scarce restrained they the people, that they had not done sacrifice unto them."*

Acts 14:19 *"And there came thither certain Jews from Antioch and Iconium, who persuaded the people, and, **having stoned Paul, drew him out of the city, supposing he had been dead**."*

Acts 14:20 *"Howbeit, **as the disciples stood round about him, he rose up, and came into the city**: and the next day he departed with Barnabas to Derbe."*

The disciples supposed Paul was dead, and I believe he actually died. 2 Corinthians 12:2-4 gives Paul's own explanation of how he was caught up to "*the third heaven*" (God's Heaven) and saw and heard many things. God sent him back for further ministry.

The Meaning Of The Third Heaven
QUESTION #1327
Genesis 1:1   *"In the beginning God created the heaven and the earth."*

Why was it called the third heaven? Is there more than one Heaven?

ANSWER #1327
Genesis 1:1 mentions both *"the heaven and the earth."* As we mention the "heavens" above us, we usually speak of three kinds:

(1)   The atmospheric heaven of the clouds

(2)   The starry heaven of the stars

(3)   The Heaven of all heavens which is God's dwelling place

I believe this third "Heaven" was called by Paul, *"the third Heaven"* which is God's dwelling place and where genuine Christians go when they die.

Meaning Of "Spirit" And "spirit"
QUESTION #1328
What would be the difference or significance between "Spirit" and "spirit"?

ANSWER #1328
1 Corinthians 12:13   *"For by one **Spirit** are we all baptized into one body, whether we be Jews or Gentiles, whether we be bond or free; and have been all made to drink into one **Spirit**."*

1 Thessalonians 5:23   "And the very God of peace sanctify you wholly; and I pray God your whole **spirit** and soul and body be preserved blameless unto the coming of our Lord Jesus Christ."

"Spirit," such as in 1 Corinthians 12:13 rightly refers to God the Holy Spirit and therefore speaks of His baptism of every true Christian the second they are saved. If the spelling of the word is changed twice to *"spirit"* as Thomas Strouse erroneously does, it would mean some sort of *"enthusiasm"* rather than the Holy Spirit of God. He heretically makes this refer to water baptism rather than the baptism by God the Holy Spirit upon a person's regeneration.

In the other verse above, "spirit" refers to the human spirit which is one of the three divisions of every human being, *"spirit and soul and body."*

Meaning Of Testimony And Testify
QUESTION #1329

I have a question to ask about a sermon I am writing. I need to know if I am using the word "*testimony*" or "*testify*" properly from Acts 20:24.

> **Acts 20:24** *"But none of these things move me, neither count I my life dear unto myself, so that I might finish my course with joy, and the ministry, which I have received of the Lord Jesus, to **testify** the gospel of the grace of God."*

Can we use this term, "*testimony*," in a similar way to "*testify*" that I am a Christian in how I live? Would I be taking "*testimony*" out of context if I use it in this way?

ANSWER #1329

The Greek Word used in this verse is DIAMARTUREO. Some of the meanings for this Greek Word are:

> "*1. testify, assert, declare (Ac 8:25; 10:42; 18:5); 2. insist, emphatically state (Ac 2:40); 3. (solemnly) warn, admonish (Lk 16:28; 2Ti 2:14; 4:1)*"

Based on the meanings of "*testify, assert, and declare*," you declare and assert what you believe by what you do, see, and listen to. In that light, I think you are on track in the way you are using DIAMARTUREO.

Did Monks Guard The Scriptures?
QUESTION #1330

I am a minister and went to a Southern Baptist Seminary. There I was taught that the monks were the guardians of the Scripture, being the only ones making copies. It was stated in class that had it not been for those monks, the Scriptures would have been lost to us today, since no one else was copying them. However, over the past 4 or 5 years, I have left the Southern Baptist denomination and am part of a King-James-Bible-only (that is, without any reference to the underlying Hebrew, Aramaic, and Greek Words) Independent Baptist congregation. The more I read and study, the more I question what I was taught about the monks being the guardians of the Bible through the Dark Ages. Is this true?

ANSWER #1330

I am glad you left the Southern Baptist Church whose leaders and seminaries are presently mainly training apostates and unbelieving Bible students. The idea that the Roman Catholic Church in some way or another, either by monks or in some other way, gave us our Bible is a total lie and falsehood! These Words were given by the Lord Jesus Christ to God the Holy Spirit Who then gave them to the human writers of the Old and New Testaments. The early Christians began making copies of those original Words from the very beginning in the 1st and 2nd centuries before the Roman Catholic Church was even thought of.

Did God Divorce Israel?

QUESTION #1331

Did God divorce Israel? Please elaborate.

ANSWER #1331

Isaiah 50:1 *"Thus saith the LORD,* **Where is the bill of your mother's divorcement, whom I have put away**? *or which of my creditors is it to whom I have sold you? Behold,* **for your iniquities** *have ye sold yourselves, and for your transgressions is your mother* **put away**."

The reason for God's temporarily putting away or divorcing His people, Israel, was for their many sins.

Jeremiah 3:8 *"And I saw, when for all the causes whereby* **backsliding Israel committed adultery I had put her away, and given her a bill of divorce**; *yet her treacherous sister Judah feared not, but went and played the harlot also."*

Dates Of New Testament Books

QUESTION #1332

When was the New Testament written?

ANSWER #1332

Though the dates of the New Testament were not written in the books themselves, the suggested estimated dates given in the *Old Scofield Reference Bible* of 1917 are as follows:

Matthew--37 A.D.
Mark--57 to 63 A.D.
Luke--63 to 68 A.D.

John--85-90 A.D.
Acts--around 65 A.D.
Romans--60 A.D.
1 Corinthians--59 A.D.
2 Corinthians--60 A.D.
Galatians--60 A.D.
Ephesians--65 A.D.
Philippians--64 A.D.
Colossians--around 65 A.D.
1 Thessalonians--54 A.D.
2 Thessalonians--around 54 A.D.
1 Timothy--between the 1st & 2nd imprisonment of Paul
2 Timothy--shortly before his death, about 66 A.D.
Titus--about the same time as 1 Timothy
Philemon--about 64 A.D.
Hebrews--70 A.D.
James--about 62 A.D.
1 Peter--about 60 A.D.
2 Peter--66 A.D.
1 John--90 A.D.
2 John--90 A.D.
3 John--90 A.D.
Jude--66 A.D.
Revelation--96 A.D.

Why Books Written Late?
QUESTION #1333
I have an unbeliever asking why the books of the Bible were written so long after Christ's death? How could they be reliable being written so long after?

ANSWER #1333
The following Bible verses show the reliability and accuracy of the very Words of our Bible.

John 16:12-14 *"I have yet many things to say unto you, but ye cannot bear them now. Howbeit when he, the Spirit of truth, is come, he will guide you into all truth: for he shall not speak of himself; but whatsoever he shall hear, that shall he speak: and he will shew you things to come. He shall glorify me: for he shall receive of mine, and shall shew it unto you."*

Based on the clear teaching of the above three verses spoken by the Lord Jesus Christ, here is how the New Testament was accurately written in the Greek language:

1.   The Lord Jesus Christ gave every Word of the Bible to God the Holy Spirit.

2.   The Holy Spirit then breathed-out these Words given to Him by the Lord Jesus Christ to the human writers who wrote them down.

3.   Both the Lord Jesus Christ (God the Son) and God the Holy Spirit are infallible and make no mistakes.

These facts hold absolutely true no matter when the Words that They gave to the human writers were written down in the books of the Bible.

Meaning Of God Or Godhead
QUESTION #1334

We often say that, because of sin, our relationship is broken with God until we accept the Lord Jesus Christ as our Saviour. I thought, when you say *"God,"* you mean the Godhead. Can you define this more clearly for me?

ANSWER #1334

The Godhead would include all the Persons of the Trinity. It would include God the Father, God the Son, and God the Holy Spirit. When it is not specific, usually "God" would refer to God the Father. It should be made clear which Person of the Godhead is meant.

Easter At The Vatican
QUESTION #1335

At the Easter service at the Vatican, they were singing to Lucifer for the last two years. That is what they appear to be saying. Is this correct?

ANSWER #1335

I took 8 semester hours of Latin in the University of Michigan and received A's in these classes. Based upon my knowledge of Latin from these courses, the translation appears to be accurate. After addressing Lucifer, he sings that *"Christ your Son"* (that is, the son of Lucifer) who came back from the dead. Lucifer in Isaiah comes from the Hebrew word HEYLEL. It means *"light bearer."* LUX is light and PHERO is to bear. It does not refer to the Lord Jesus Christ, but to Satan who appears as an "angel of light" (2 Corinthians 11:14 *"And no marvel; for Satan himself is transformed into an angel of light.*") It serious heresy to make Lucifer into God Whose Son is the Lord Jesus Christ.

Lucifer The Morning Star?
QUESTION #1336

Revelation 22:16 *"I Jesus have sent mine angel to testify unto you these things in the churches. I am the root and the offspring of David, and* ***the bright and morning star****."*

Here, the Lord Jesus Christ is called the *"morning star"* and yet in one of the Latin statements from the Roman Catholic Church, it refers to Lucifer or Satan as the *"morning star."* Is this correct?

ANSWER #1336

*Flammas eius **lúcifer** matutínus invéniat:*
*ille, inquam, **lúcifer**, qui nescit occásum.*
Christus Fílius tuus*,*
qui, regréssus ab ínferis,
humáno géneri serénus illúxit,
et vivit et regnat in sæcula sæculórum.

"May this flame be found still burning
*by the **Morning Star**:*
*the one **Morning Star** who never sets,*
Christ your Son*,*
who, coming back from death's domain,
has shed his peaceful light on humanity,
and lives and reigns for ever and ever."

In Latin, Lucifer is the name given by Roman astronomers to the Morning Star, the bright planet seen in the dawn sky. We know it by another Roman name–Venus. Lucifer actually comes from the Latin term *'lucem ferre,'* meaning "the bearer of light," and (the star) Venus was called this because it appeared in the sky just before the sun. The symbolism was that Venus (the star called Lucifer) was the herald that announced the arrival of the sun in the morning.

Revelation 22:16   *"**I Jesus** have sent mine angel to testify unto you these things in the churches. **I am the** root and the offspring of David, and the bright and **morning star**."*

In the Bible, the Lord Jesus Christ is called *"the Morning Star."* It cannot be a title for Lucifer who is Satan himself!

Meaning Of Glory And Glorified
QUESTION #1337

I was wondering if you could shed some light on the words "*glory*" and "*glorified.*"

ANSWER #1337

Here are 11 shades of the meaning of "*glory*" from a Greek dictionary.

> "*1. splendor, glory (1Pe 1:24); 2. brightness, shining, radiance (Ac 22:11; Rev 15:8); 3. amazing might, demonstration of power (Ro 6:4); 4. praise, speak words of honor and glory (Lk 17:18; Jn 9:24); 5. honor, give an assignment of status (Lk 14:10); 6. greatness, the state of being wonderful (Mt 4:8; 12:27); 7. glorious being, benevolent supernatural power (2Pe 2:10); 8. heaven, a glorious place (1Ti 3:16); 9. pride, the reason or basis for legitimate pride (1Th 2:20); 10. promise to tell truth, formally, give glory to God (Jn 9:24+), for another interp, see "praise"; 11. the Sublime Glory, the Majestic Glory (2Pe 1:17+)*"

Meaning Of Soul And Spirit
QUESTION #1338

I have a question regarding our recent Bible reading out of Revelation 16:3 "*And the second angel poured out his vial upon the sea, and it became as the blood of a dead man: and **every living soul died in the sea.**" Question: So, animals have a "soul" but not a "spirit"? Man is the only one that has a "spirit"?

I also noticed in our current reading in Genesis 2:7 "*And the LORD God formed man of the dust of the ground, and breathed into his nostrils the breath of life, and **man became a living soul.**"

What is the distinction between these two verses? They both (creatures and man) refer to being a *living soul*?

ANSWER #1338

The Greek Word for living "*soul*" is PSYCHE. The Hebrew Word for living "*soul*" is NEPHESH. Both words are used for "LIVING" although sometimes they refer to the inner soul which speaks of feelings. This is true of 1 Thessalonians 5:23. Many have given definitions to "soul" and "spirit" and "body." The soul has to do with our emotions and feelings. In this definition, animals have feelings and so have "souls" in this sense, though they do not have spirits. The spirit has to do with that part of us (if saved) that can communicate with the Lord. The body is our physical part of us. Animals have bodies also. Lost people have feelings (souls) and spirits (though dead to God) and bodies. When people are genuine Christians, they have God's Holy Spirit indwelling them in addition to having their human spirit, and soul, and body. When we speak of "soul winning," we're speaking of seeking to win a person's dead "spirit" into eternal life.

> **1 Thessalonians 5:23** *"And the very God of peace sanctify you wholly; and I pray God **your whole spirit and soul and body** be preserved blameless unto the coming of our Lord Jesus Christ."*

Jehovah vs. Yahweh

QUESTION #1339

I was reading an article today in the *Zion's Fire* by Marvin Rosenthal. He mentioned that "when God revealed His proper name YAHWEH (erroneously translated JEHOVAH) to Moses, He said, *"This is my name for ever"* (Exodus 3:13-15). What is your answer about the translation JEHOVAH?

ANSWER #1339

I realize that many have changed the spelling of God's Old Testament Name from JEHOVAH to YAHWEH, but the literal transliteration (letter for letter) of the Hebrew Word in the Hebrew Old Testament is JE-HO-VAH. The Hebrew letter YODH can be transliterated as either a "J" or a "Y." The Hebrew letter VAU can be transliterated either "V" or "W." If you remove the Hebrew vowels that are in that Hebrew Word, you would get JHVH OR YHWH.

In every Hebrew Bible, the vowel points are present in all seven of the verses below, showing that the correct pronunciation according to God's Words (not man's ideas) is JEHOVAH and not YAHWEH, whatever Marvin Rosenthal or any other modern or ancient person might say about it. I also disagree with Marvin Rosenthal in his hatred for the clear teachings of the New Testament about the pre-Tribulation Rapture by the Lord Jesus Christ of all the saved ones before any part of the Tribulation begins.

> **Genesis 22:14** *"And Abraham called the name of that place **Jehovahjireh**: as it is said to this day, In the mount of the LORD it shall be seen."*

> **Exodus 6:3**   *"And I appeared unto Abraham, unto Isaac, and unto Jacob, by the name of God Almighty, but by my name **Jehovah** was I not known to them."*

> **Exodus 17:15** *"And Moses built an altar, and called the name of it **Jehovahnissi**:"*

> **Judges 6:24** *"Then Gideon built an altar there unto the LORD, and called it **Jehovahshalom**: unto this day it is yet in Ophrah of the Abiezrites."*

> **Psalms 83:18** *"That men may know that thou, whose name alone is **Jehovah**, art the most high over all the earth."*

> **Isaiah 12:2** *"Behold, God is my salvation; I will trust, and not be afraid: for the LORD **JEHOVAH** is my strength and my song; he also is become my salvation."*

> **Isaiah 26:4**   *"Trust ye in the LORD for ever: for in the LORD **JEHOVAH** is everlasting strength:"*

Meaning Of Neesings Or Sneezings
QUESTION #1340

What is your position on Job 41:18? Most King James Bibles use "*neesings,*" but a few use "*sneezings.*" Why are they different?

ANSWER #1340

First of all, you should use the proper King James Bible and not go by how the other so-called King James Bibles word things. The proper one is used by our *Defined King James Bible*. It is the one authorized by the Cambridge University Press. It had a kind of copyright in 1611 when it was printed. It was called *cum privilegio.* When the United States began to publish the King James Bibles, they did not accept this copyright and have been changing the King James Bible wording ever since. You can't trust the King James Bibles published by Zondervan, Moody, Nelson, or any of the other publishers. You should only go by the King James Bibles published by the Cambridge University Press such as we do in our *Defined King James Bible.*   My LOGOS Bible program gives these Hebrew meanings for ATISA: *"sneezing, scream, or shriek."*

Paragraphs In The Bible
QUESTION #1341

I would like to know if the paragraphs in the Bible are in the originals, and if so, which Bibles have the correct paragraphs.

ANSWER #1341

In the original Old Testament Hebrew and Aramaic and in the original Greek New Testament, there were no paragraphs.   There were only words and sentences.   Also, there were no verses.   These were inserted much later.   I don't know which Bibles have the correct paragraphs.   It was the only the opinion of the publishers where they inserted the verses or paragraphs.

Walking After Flesh–Saved?
QUESTION #1342

Can people who seem to be walking after their flesh be genuine Christians?

ANSWER #1342

Since born-again genuine Christians (as well as every unsaved person) still have their old, sinful, wicked flesh with them until they die, they are capable–though disobedient in doing so--(if they walk after their flesh rather than after the power of God the Holy Spirit Who indwells them) to commit any of the list of the 17+ works of the flesh listed below as mentioned in Galatians 5:19-21.   They should not manifest any of these works of the flesh, but Paul would not have listed them to the Galatians if once they were saved they could not commit any of them.

As far as people being *"practicing homosexuals,"* though it might be possible for them to be true Christians, it would seem quite unlikely. Once practicing homosexuals would become true Christians, they should immediately stop that wickedness and live pure lives for the Lord Jesus Christ.

> **Galatians 5:19** *"Now the works of the flesh are manifest, which are these; Adultery, fornication, uncleanness, lasciviousness,"*
> **Galatians 5:20** *"Idolatry, witchcraft, hatred, variance, emulations, wrath, strife, seditions, heresies,"*

Galatians 5:21 *"Envyings, murders, drunken-ness, revellings, and such like: of the which I tell you before, as I have also told you in time past, that they which do such things shall not inherit the kingdom of God."*

When people are walking after their flesh, it is difficult to figure out if they are (1) lost and bound for Hell, or (2) saved and bound for Heaven, but walking after their sinful flesh nature rather than being led by God the Holy Spirit Who indwells them. Only God Himself knows for sure the spiritual status of such people.

Meaning Of Proverbs 30:17
QUESTION #1343

Exactly what is that verse saying? Is it more literal or more figurative? And is it more punitive or is it more corrective?

Proverbs 30:17 *"The eye that mocketh at his father, and despiseth to obey his mother, the ravens of the valley shall pick it out, and the young eagles shall eat it."*

ANSWER #1343

As for Proverbs 30:17, I would just take it as meaning that there will be very, very severe consequences for a son or daughter who mocks and despises his or her father and mother. I would take the ravens and young eagles as figures of speech in this verse, indicating the severity of God's judgment in such a case.

The Meaning Of John 3:15
QUESTION #1344

I have a question on John 3.15. My question I have is on the "only *begotten Son.*" In the footnotes 3b you have translated *"Uniquely related."* New versions have that same translation and many KJV advocates are upset that they replaced the original writing as *"uniquely related."* Could you please help me understand why it was translated *"uniquely related"*?

ANSWER #1344

In the first place, *"only begotten"* does not appear in John 3:15. It is in John 3:16. Our *Defined King James Bible* does not *"translate"* it in any other fashion than what is in the text, that is, *"only begotten."* The footnotes merely give other meanings to the words. They are not *"translations."* We do not make, or even suggest, any changes in the *"translation"* found in the King James Bible.

Meaning of The Year Of Jubilee
QUESTION #1345

In *"the year of jubilee"* (jubile) does this mean the land is restored to the original owner without cost?

ANSWER #1345

Though it is not crystal clear, it seems from these 3 sections of Leviticus 25 that in the year of jubilee, the original owner returns to his own possession without paying for it. It was just on loan for 50 years for others to work their land and bring in all the fruits. But the land itself returns after the 50 years were up so that, in the long run, no one ever loses their own land. The verses below seem to teach this.

> **Leviticus 25:10** *"And ye shall hallow the fiftieth year, and proclaim liberty throughout all the land unto all the inhabitants thereof: it shall be a jubile unto you; and ye shall return every man unto his possession, and ye shall return every man unto his family."*

> **Leviticus 25:28** *"But if he be not able to restore it to him, then that which is sold shall remain in the hand of him that hath bought it until the year of jubile: and in the jubile it shall go out, and he shall return unto his possession."*

> **Leviticus 25:40** *"But as an hired servant, and as a sojourner, he shall be with thee, and shall serve thee unto the year of jubile:"*

> **Leviticus 25:41** *'And then shall he depart from thee, both he and his children with him, and shall return unto his own family, and unto the possession of his fathers shall he return.'*

> **Leviticus 25:54** *"And if he be not redeemed in these years, then he shall go out in the year of jubile, both he, and his children with him."*

Matthias Or Paul Replaced Judas?
QUESTION #1346
Did Paul replace Judas as the 12th Apostle?
ANSWER #1346
Though others differ on this question, I believe that Paul was the person, chosen by the Lord Jesus Christ to replace Judas Iscariot, the traitor. Here are some verses that make this clear.

1.   **Galatians 1:1** "***Paul, an apostle***, (not of men, neither by man, but **by Jesus Christ**, and God the Father, who raised him from the dead;)" This clearly teaches that Paul was made an apostle by Jesus Christ Himself. Matthias was not chosen by the Lord Jesus Christ, but only by Peter and the others with him.

2.   **Galatians 1:19** "*But other of the apostles saw I none, save James the Lord's brother.*" This does not deny that Paul was an "*apostle,*" but "*other of the apostles*" implies that he is also an "*apostle.*"

3.   **Romans 1:1** "*Paul, a servant of Jesus Christ, called to be an apostle, separated unto the gospel of God,*" This verse is very clear that the Lord Jesus Christ Himself called Paul to be an "*apostle.*" He was not made one by picking one of the two nominees put up by Peter before the descent of God the Holy Spirit for Whom Christ ordered His leaders to "*wait.*"

> **Acts 1:4** "*And, being assembled together with them, commanded them that they should not depart from Jerusalem, but **wait for the promise of the Father**, which, saith he, ye have heard of me.*"

They failed to "*wait*" for the descent of God the Holy Spirit, but instead held an election. As such, Peter was off base as he was many other times in the Gospel records.

There is another verse where Paul himself uses the expression, "*us the apostles*" which included Paul with all of the other apostles who were chosen by the Lord Jesus Christ Himself.

> **1 Corinthians 4:9** "For I think that God hath set forth **us the apostles** last, as it were appointed to death: for we are made a spectacle unto the world, and to angels, and to men."

Meaning Of Balaam's Orders
QUESTION #1347

Pastor, I have a question regarding our daily reading in Numbers 22. It appears in verse 13, that Balaam was told of God not to go with these men, but the second time they came back (with more honorable men) to him to bid him to come to Balak. Balaam thought to ask the Lord again what he should do. In verse 21, the Lord told him to "*rise and go with them*" but in verse 22, God's anger was kindled against him because he went. Was this because that Balaam once again asked what the Lord would have him to do, even though the Lord clearly had told him once before "not" to go with them? Why would the Lord have told him to go and then be angry that he did go?

ANSWER #1347

I believe God's "permissive will" and God's "directive will" are different. God's "directive will" and "perfect will" for Balaam was for him not to go to pagan Balak. It is only His "permissive will" that allowed him to go, but not without God's chastisement on him because he was out of the "direct" and "perfect" will of God. He used the ass to chasten and protect him from the angel of God that was going to slay him for being out of the "directive" and "perfect" will of God. There are three New Testament verses that shed light on the wickedness of Balaam:

> **2 Peter 2:15** "*Which have **forsaken the right way, and are gone astray, following the way of Balaam the son of Bosor, who loved the wages of unrighteousness**;*"

> **Jude 1:11** "***Woe unto them! for they have** gone in the way of Cain, and **ran greedily after the error of Balaam for reward**, and perished in the gainsaying of Core.*"

> **Revelation 2:14** "*But **I have a few things against thee, because thou hast there them that hold the doctrine of Balaam, who taught Balac to cast a stumblingblock before the children of Israel, to eat things sacrificed unto idols, and to commit fornication**.*"

From these verses, you can see what a wicked and sinful man Balaam was.

Meaning Of Blood Moons

QUESTION #1348

There is a pastor on the Internet named Pastor Biltz. He speaks of four Blood moons. Is he correct in his predictions?

ANSWER #1348

I think Pastor Biltz and others who follow him on the blood moons prophecy to signify the soon Rapture of the genuine Christians have the entire prophetic picture wrong.

1.   The prophecies in Joel and Acts take place "*before the great and terrible day of the LORD come*" which is **after** the seven-year Tribulation, not before the Tribulation or before the Rapture of all true Christians by the Lord Jesus Christ.

2.   In both Joel and in Acts, "**the sun shall be turned into darkness**" which is entirely left out of the "blood moon" prophecies.

3.   In both Joel and Acts, this will be a Divinely-performed special miracle! It will not come from a natural phenomenon of what happens in nature about blood moons. God will do it supernaturally, and not merely naturally as Biltz and his followers proclaim.

4.   In short, I believe this entire blood moon prophecy is blatant heresy and contrary to the Bible's clear teachings.

5.   It is sad that many, many people are falling for this blood moon nonsense, and are being deceived by it. This is true even of a man I know very well.

> Joel 2:31   '*The sun shall be turned into darkness, and the moon into blood, before the great and the terrible day of the LORD come.*"
>
> Joel 3:15 "*The sun and the moon shall be darkened, and the stars shall withdraw their shining.*"
>
> Acts 2:20   "*The sun shall be turned into darkness, and the moon into blood, before that great and notable day of the Lord come:*"

The Writer Of Hebrews

QUESTION #1349

I wanted to know something about the epistle to the Hebrews. Do you think Paul was the writer?

ANSWER #1349

I make clear that I believe it was Paul who was the writer of Hebrews in the first chapter of my book, *Hebrews–Preaching Verse-By-Verse* (**BFT #4046 @ $30.00 + $8.00 S&H**). I give the following five reasons for this belief:

In this book of Hebrews, we see **five reasons** why **Paul** is the writer. It was written about 64 A.D., probably between the first and second Roman imprisonments. But many people doubt that it was **Paul**, because **Paul** did not put his name on it.

1. The first reason I believe it is **Paul,** is that **Paul** wrote to the Jews in the dispersion according to 2 Peter 3:15.

> **2 Peter 3:15**
> *"And account that the longsuffering of our Lord is salvation; even as our beloved brother **Paul** also according to the wisdom given unto him **hath written unto you;"***

Paul as well as Peter wrote to the Jews who were converted to Christ.

2. The second reason is, **the style is that of Paul**. The words, the style, and the flow are **Pauline.**

> **Hebrews 13:23**
> *"Know ye that **our** brother **Timothy is set at liberty**; with whom, if he come shortly, I will see you."*

He talks about liberty. He talks about being in prison. He knows about that.

3. The third reason is, **he talks about the saints of Italy**. He knew who was there in Italy, because **he was in Rome as a prisoner**.

> **Hebrews 13:24**
> *"Salute all them that have the rule over you, and **all the saints. They of Italy salute you**."*

He is apparently writing this from Italy. This could be a prison epistle itself.

4. The fourth reason is, he knows something about bonds—being enslaved in bonds.

> **Hebrews 10:34**
> *"For **ye had compassion of me in my bonds**, and took joyfully the spoiling of your goods, knowing in yourselves that ye have in heaven a better and an enduring substance."*

They knew that he was in prison.

> **Hebrews 13:3**
> *"**Remember them that are in bonds**, as bound with them; and them which suffer adversity, as being yourselves also in the body."*

5. The fifth reason is, **Paul holds the traditional authorship** that is found in the Greek text. It is given in the old Scofield Bible. It is given in many places. I do not know why these newcomers say that Paul did not write Hebrews. I believe he did.

What Is The Source Of Philemon?
QUESTION #1350
I was trying to verify some of the footnotes in my Bible, such as the footnote at the end of Philemon which says that it was written by Onesimus. What does this mean?

ANSWER #1350
When the note says "*written by Onesimus*," it means that he was the stenographer to whom Paul dictated the letter. I believe Paul was the writer, and Onesimus was the stenographer.

Easter In Acts 12:1-4?
QUESTION #1351
Should "*Easter*" be in Acts 12:1-4 in our King James Bible?

ANSWER #1351
It is true that Ishtar and Easter are pagan and unbiblical. This reference might have been referring to such a pagan feast which was going on at that time. It would be a faulty translation to use the word, "Passover" in Acts 12:4 since this was at the time of the days of unleavened bread (the 15th day of the first month) and Passover, being on the 14th day of that month, had already passed.

> **Acts 12:1** *"Now about that time Herod the king stretched forth his hands to vex certain of the church."*
> **Acts 12:2** *"And he killed James the brother of John with the sword."*
> **Acts 12:3** *"And because he saw it pleased the Jews, he proceeded further to take Peter also. (**Then were the days of unleavened bread**.)"*
> **Acts 12:4** *"And when he had apprehended him, he put him in prison, and delivered him to four quaternions of soldiers to keep him; **intending after Easter to bring him forth to the people**."*
> **Leviticus 23:5** *"**In the fourteenth day of the first month at even is the LORD'S passover**."*
> **Leviticus 23:6** *"And **on the fifteenth day of the same month is the feast of unleavened bread** unto the LORD: seven days ye must eat unleavened bread."*

Source Of 1 Corinthians?

QUESTION #1352

Did Paul write the letter of 1 Corinthians from Philippi, or Ephesus?

ANSWER #1352

It is not known for sure, but indications are that 1 Corinthians was written from Ephesus about 59 A.D. Paul was at Ephesus for around three years. 2 Corinthians was probably written about 60 A.D. from Philippi. Places of origin, unless clearly stated in the verses themselves, are unknown for certain. They are only speculations.

Two On The Road To Emmaus

QUESTION #1353

Is there any thing in the Greek language that would indicate the gender of the second disciple of Jesus, who with Cleopas, walked with Jesus on the road to Emmaus?

ANSWER #1353

There is no way to tell whether one was the wife of Cleopas or another man. Cleopas is masculine, but there is no way to distinguish "*they*," and "*them*" I always had thought they were two men until Mrs. Waite and I went to the Holy Land. On our tour, we visited Emmaus. The pictures on the wall of that church were that of a man and a woman, probably Cleopas and his wife. That made sense to me, though there is no verse to back it up.

Who Arose First?

QUESTION #1354

Matthew 27:50 "*Jesus, when he had cried again with a loud voice, yielded up the ghost.*"

Matthew 27:51 "*And, behold, the veil of the temple was rent in twain from the top to the bottom; and the earth did quake, and the rocks rent;*"

Matthew 27:52 "*And the graves were opened; and **many bodies of the saints which slept arose**,*"

Matthew 27:53 "***And came out of the graves after his resurrection**, and went into the holy city, and appeared unto many.*"

In the interpretation of Matthew 27:50-53, there are two

positions. Which one is correct? (1) One side says that when Jesus died, the graves opened, and dead people rose again. (2) The other side says the dead people rose again first, then Jesus rose again. Can you explain this more clearly?

ANSWER #1354

I think the clear teaching is that the Lord Jesus Christ died first. After His death, the veil of the temple was rent, the earth quaked, and the rocks were rent. After Christ's bodily resurrection, the graves were opened, and many bodies arose, came out of the graves, and appeared to many. There is a gap of three days and three nights between Christ's death and His bodily resurrection just like there is a gap of three days and three nights before these graves were opened and the bodies came out.

That Which Is Perfect & Sign Gifts

QUESTION #1355

1 **Corinthians 13:8** "*Charity never faileth: but whether there be prophecies, **they shall fail**; whether there be tongues, **they shall cease**; whether there be knowledge, **it shall vanish away**.*"

1 **Corinthians 13:9** "*For we know in part, and we prophesy in part.*"

1 **Corinthians 13:10** "*But when that which is perfect is come, then that which is in part **shall be done away**.*"

In 1 Corinthians 13:10 "*But when **that which is perfect** is come, then that which is in part shall be done away,*" what does "*that which is perfect*" mean?

ANSWER #1355

Regarding the meaning of "*that which is perfect*" in 1 Corinthians 13:10, there are two things to keep in mind:'

1.   It does not mean "**He** *Who is perfect*" referring to a masculine person or to the coming of the Lord Jesus Christ, because the Greek gender is not masculine but is neuter. It would be grammatically impossible for it to refer to a masculine person of any kind.

2.   The Greek Words involved in the English translation "*that which is perfect*" are TO TELEION (which is neuter, not masculine). It must therefore refer to a neuter noun such as TO BIBLION ("the Bible"). I believe that is the Greek neuter noun reference here. The meaning is "*when the Bible has been completed*," the sign gifts

mentioned (and all the others in the New Testament) will cease. The Bible was completed around 90 or 100 A.D. At that time, four things happened to these sign gifts and all the others mentioned in the New Testament--they **failed**, they **ceased**, they **vanished away**, and they **were done away**. This is the Biblical answer to the errors of the Charismatic and Pentecostal movements.

Meaning of "Never Knew You"
QUESTION #1356

In Matthew 7:21-23 the Lord Jesus Christ uses the term, "*I never knew you.*" That is a very scary verse. What is the meaning of the word, "*knew*" in this verse? *How can we be sure it never applies to any of us?*

ANSWER #1356

Matthew 7:23   "And then will I profess unto them, **I never knew you**: depart from me, ye that work iniquity."

In the context, the Lord Jesus Christ was saying that it is not enough for people who call Him "*Lord*" to be certain of Heaven. It must be followed by genuinely trusting the Lord Jesus Christ as their Saviour. If this is true, He will never say "*I never knew you.*"

Meaning Of Various Verses
QUESTION #1357

I would like to find our your point of view on the following verses:

1.   Do you believe that 1 John 5:7-8 is inspired Scripture and belongs in the King James Bible?

2.   Do you believe that "Easter" instead of "Passover" is the correct term in Acts 12:4?

3.   Do you believe that the text of the King James Bible can be fully interpreted from its English text without the need to refer to the Hebrew, Aramaic, or Greek?

ANSWER #1357

1.   I believe 1 John 5:7-8 are proper verses that should remain in our New Testament. We have several materials defending these verses that are available from our Bible For Today catalog below:
        http://biblefortoday.org/idx_Pages/idx_catalog.htm

2.   I believe Acts 12:4 should remain as "*Easter*" meaning the pagan feast celebrated by the heathen around the same time as the Jewish "*Passover.*" If it were translated "*passover,*" there would be a huge contradiction because it was already the 15th day of the first

month being the feast of unleavened bread. The Passover had occurred the day before on the 14ᵗʰ day of the first month. Because of this, it would be inconsistent to put *"Passover"* in place of *"Easter"* in the clause, *"intending after Easter to bring him forth to the people."* Passover had already occurred on the 14ᵗʰ day of the first month.

   3.   The full and complete interpretation of the New Testament should be by a comparison of the King James Bible English with the Hebrew, Aramaic, and Greek preserved original, and inspired Words. If people have no knowledge of the original language Words, they can get help by consulting lexicons (dictionaries) and grammars to help in these details.

The Meaning Of Psalm 1
QUESTION #1358

   In Psalm 1, it says: *"Blessed is the man ..."* When it says *"man"* does it mean only male? Or is it also speaking of both man and woman? My wife is trying to translate the King James Bible into the Finnish language, but wanted to know whether *"blessed is the man,"* as in Psalm 1 or in the Sermon on the Mount, is a masculine gender, or does it includes women also?

ANSWER #1358

   The Hebrew word for "*man*" in Psalm 1:1 is masculine, but it implies both men and women. "*Man*" is used in the sense of someone in the huMAN race, or a member of MANkind.

   The Greek for "*men*" in Matthew 6:1 is ANTHROPOS which is masculine, but includes both men and women. ANER is the Greek Word which is exclusively male. Often when our King James Bible has "*man,*" it is a translation for the Greek Word "TIS" which means "*someone,*" either male or female, though the King James Bible in 1611 used the word "*man*" for "TIS." This was a customary use in that day and culture.

Capitalization In Bible Verses
QUESTION #1359

   We got into a little discussion at Bible study last week about the capitalization of the word "Today" and none of us have been able to figure it out. Could you please briefly tell us why in Hebrews sometimes Today is capitalized and other times it isn't?

ANSWER #1359

Below are the 6 uses of "*to day*" in the book of Hebrews. The "T" is capitalized because it is a quote from the O.T. in 3:7, 3:15, 4:7, and

5:5. That's why it's "T." I don't know the reason for 3:13. It is small "t" in 13:8 because there is no quote.

Hebrews 3:7 "*Wherefore (as the Holy Ghost saith, **To day** if ye will hear his voice,*"

Hebrews 3:13 "*But exhort one another daily, while it is called **To day**; lest any of you be hardened through the deceitfulness of sin.*"

Hebrews 3:15 "*While it is said, **To day** if ye will hear his voice, harden not your hearts, as in the provocation.*"

Hebrews 4:7 "*Again, he limiteth a certain day, saying in David, **To day**, after so long a time; as it is said, To day if ye will hear his voice, harden not your hearts.*"

Hebrews 5:5 "*So also Christ glorified not himself to be made an high priest; but he that said unto him, Thou art my Son, **to day** have I begotten thee.*"

Hebrews 13:8 "*Jesus Christ the same yesterday, and **to day**, and for ever.*"

The Meaning Of Hebrews 6:4-6

QUESTION #1360

Hebrews 6:4 "*For it is impossible for those who were once **enlightened**, and have **tasted of the heavenly gift**, and were **made partakers of the Holy Ghost**,*"

Hebrews 6:5 "*And have **tasted the good word of God**, and the powers of the world to come,*"

Hebrews 6:6 "*If they shall fall away, to renew them again unto repentance; seeing they crucify to themselves the Son of God afresh, and put him to an open shame.*"

I have a question concerning Hebrew 6:4-6. What are these verses talking about?

ANSWER #1360

I have taken a strong position on this in my messages on Hebrews. Here's the LINK in audio format that I used also in my Hebrews book:

(http://www.sermonaudio.com/sermoninfo.asp?SID=128131517320)

In simple terms, no one can ever lose their genuine salvation once they have it. They can drift into carnality and worldliness if they walk after their sinful flesh rather than in the power and leadership of God the Holy Spirit Who indwells them. It seems clear, because of the terms used of them, that those mentioned in these Hebrews verses were genuine Christians who were well-versed in the Bible truths. But they refused to return to His fellowship after living in sin for so long. They did not practice 1 John 1:9 and be restored to God's fellowship. In these cases many times they have committed the sin unto physical death as mentioned in 1 John 5:16, and God just takes them Home to Heaven because of their disgrace to His Name.

1 John 5:16 *"If any man see his brother sin a sin which is not unto death, he shall ask, and he shall give him life for them that sin not unto death. There is a sin unto death: I do not say that he shall pray for it."*

Meaning Of Revelation 22:18-19

QUESTION #1361

Revelation 22:18 *"For I testify unto every man that heareth the words of the prophecy of this book, If any man shall **add unto these things, God shall add unto him the plagues** that are written in this book:"*

Revelation 22:19 *"And if any man shall **take away from the words** of the book of this prophecy, **God shall take away his part** out of the book of life, and out of the holy city, and from the things which are written in this book."*

What does *"this book"* refer to? Revelation, or the entire Bible?

ANSWER #1361

I believe that "*this book*" would mean the book of Revelation, but since that is the last book of the Bible written in 90 or 100 A.D., it would refer to any of the Bible books. I believe that no Words of the Bible should be added to, subtracted, or changed in any other way. *The Book of Mormon* has done this as well as *Science And Health*

With The Key To The Scriptures which Christian Science has done. Many Bibles in all different languages add, subtract, and otherwise change God's Hebrew, Aramaic, and Greek Words.

I believe the taking away of this person's *"part"* would refer to his reward that he shall have forfeited by removing some of God's Words from the Bible as many modern translators have done.

CHAPTER X
QUESTIONS ABOUT
CONSTITUTIONAL FREEDOMS

Impeachment of Federal Workers
QUESTION #1362
Should officials who serve in our federal government, under the rules and principles of our United States Constitution, ever be impeached?

ANSWER #1362
When it has been shown that such a public official has committed what our United States Constitution calls "*high crimes and misdemeanors,*" that official should be impeached. It is sad to see our Constitution being violated in many, many ways in recent years. Where will it all end? The constitution should be followed meticulously throughout its regulations, including impeachment where called for.

Martial Law And Obama
QUESTION #1363
I do not believe that this is going to happen. There are some people who are trying to stir up problems. There were people caught doing it. There was something on the news a couple of days ago that there were 2 people who shot 2 police officers in a pizza restaurant and screamed that that was the start of a revolution and then went to Walmart and shot each other. And then, the FEMA scare was being circulated on the internet for so long, so, I did a research on that and it turned out to be false; actually Glenn Beck ran an investigation on it and disproved it.

ANSWER #1363
I wish you were correct in this, but all the evidence seems to point to a time when Obama will declare, even in peacetime, martial law. This will close down all elections, and will turn our nation into a land similar to Hitler's Germany and Stalin's Russia.

I ask you to read again very carefully Obama's recent **Executive Order #13603** to see how all of this is going to take place. This is one of the reasons why Obama's various departments have amassed billions of rounds of ammunition and more than 2,000 tank-like vehicles--waiting to turn on the crowds who will be rioting in the streets when their food stamps stop and they have no money because the banks have closed.

Obama's planned invasion of hundreds of people across the border, including many children, is helping to turn our great nation into a socialist, government-run state.   This will grind our Constitutional freedoms to a halt as we run out of food for them, hospital care for them, homes, and everything else. This is all part of his grandiose plans to further his dictatorship over us.

I am enclosing a PDF of Obama's **Executive Order #13603** whereby he plans to be President forever. The EO #13603 is written so that he, the President, can give the command, to turn our country into Martial Law. He can use the help of Russian and Chinese troops that are now in our country, training for this purpose. His plan for Martial law is why he had to fire hundreds of faithful military generals and admirals and others of high rank because they would refuse to fire upon our own American citizens when breaking up the riots which will come. I wish this would not be the case, but all evidence points very loudly in this direction. Time alone will tell, but no one knows when the time will come.

Churches And IRS Tax Exemption
QUESTION #1364

I notice that the noose is starting to tighten around churches over this incorporation thing. I was wondering what your thoughts are about the church and incorporation, employee withholdings, workers compensation, and similar things.

ANSWER #1364

The IRS seems to be cracking down since they have been censoring conservative groups of all kinds. I believe we must continue to stand for all the Bible principles, regardless what the IRS does to us. Incorporation keeps someone from suing every member of the church if a suit is filed. Incorporation means there will be only one defendant, should a suit happen. That is helpful. I think withholding and workers compensation are up to each church to determine.

Military Leaders And Obama

QUESTION #1365

Did Obama dismiss many high-ranking officers in the U. S. Army, Navy, and Marine Corps recently? Why was that?

ANSWER #1365

It is my understanding that the military officers that Obama now has will cooperate with whatever he wishes of them. The Generals, Admirals and other top military men who refused to agree to fire on U. S. citizens in case of martial law or other disorders were dismissed by Obama. The military leaders now in place will do whatever Obama tells them to do. I hope you read every word of the article entitled "Obama President Forever." It describes his latest unconstitutional Executive Order setting up his dictatorial rule over America.

Will FEMA Camps Be Coming?

QUESTION #1366

The FEMA camp scare was being circulated on the internet for so long, so I did some research on it. I found this scare to be false. Do you agree?

ANSWER #1366

I wish you were correct in this, but all the evidence seems to point to a time when Obama will declare, even in peacetime, martial law. When this takes place, those who resist Obama's dictatorship will be placed in FEMA prison camps so they can be controlled. There are many such FEMA camps already set up around our country preparing to imprison those who will not succumb to rules contrary to our United States Constitution.

BFTBC & Constitutional Stands

QUESTION #1367

Should churches be involved in our country's Constitutional freedoms?

ANSWER #1367

One of the amendments in our United States Constitution concerns the "free exercise of religion" and "freedom of speech." Our Bible-believing churches such as our own Bible For Today Baptist Church has every right to maintain information and support to maintain these (and many others) two freedoms. Without these freedoms, the gospel of the Lord Jesus Christ cannot go out freely and without interruption. It might not be in the too-distant future when these freedoms and many others will cease to be present in our

United States of America. As a pastor, I am commanded to "watch" as well as "warn." This I will continue to do to the best of my abilities. I intend to continue: (1) to stand for the King James Bible and the Words of God in the Hebrew, Aramaic, and Greek underlying the King James Bible as well as oppose and refute the Gnostic Critical Text modern translations and theology that stand against these Words, and (2) to stand for the principles of the United States Constitution and oppose and refute all individuals and groups who oppose this U. S. Constitution and the freedoms it safeguards.

Church Discussing The President
QUESTION #1368
Should pastors refer to President Obama in their comments on the Bible?

ANSWER #1368
As I explain in the comment below, I believe it is my task as a pastor, not only to preach and teach the Words of God, but also to warn genuine Christians about the conditions in our country and in the world that we face which are out to destroy our rights to preach the Words of God. President Obama should be exposed by godly Pastors for his many lies and deceits that he says repeatedly about many different topics as well as his many violations of the United States Constitution by means of his unconstitutional Executive Orders and his other violations of the Constitution's clear directives. I believe it is one of my tasks to warn our fellow born-again Christians of what we might well be facing in the weeks, months, and years to come right in this country, including fines, imprisonment, and even death. Our heads must not be in the sand in matters of our freedoms in our country or the dwindling down of the same by our federal, state, or local governments.

501c3 And The IRS
QUESTION #1369
Is tax exemption for 501C3 churches only, or for all churches in our country?

ANSWER #1369
I do not believe this government tax-exempt status applies only to 501c-3 churches. It applies to all churches. Many states give tax exemption to all churches, not only those who are under 501c-3.

A Constitutional Convention

QUESTION #1370

Do you favor a Constitutional Convention to amend our present Constitution?

ANSWER #1370

A Constitutional Convention for whatever amendment people might think is good is an extremely foolish thing to do. Once the Convention convenes, Obama and his followers will further eliminate all the good things presently in our Constitution. If they don't keep our present Constitutional principles, why do you think they will keep other provisions that might be added? This would be used to trash even the present Constitutional provisions.   I know many conservatives are in favor of calling for this, but they should be totally against it.

Martial Law Elimination?

QUESTION #1371

Is there any possible way that Congress can stop martial law from happening?

ANSWER #1371

By his unconstitutional Executive Order, Obama gave himself the exclusive authority to put martial law into effect for any reason he might use.   Congress could declare his Executive Order unconstitutional, but they do not have any unity in a desire to try to restore all the provisions of the United States Constitution. In view of this, it doesn't look like Congress will undo Obama's dictatorial power to institute martial law in this country any time he wishes. This is a sad condition to be in.

CHAPTER XI
QUESTIONS ABOUT
MISCELLANEOUS SUBJECTS

What's Going On In China?
QUESTION #1372
Do you know what is happening these days in China?
ANSWER #1372
There is over a trillion dollar debt in China now. Many homes in China are empty. In some cities it is one out of five such homes, according to some data. There also is evidence that there are Chinese soldiers right now within the USA.

The Tribulation And Israel
QUESTION #1373
I have a friend that is struggling with what is going on in the world, and she believes that if this treaty is signed in Israel, very soon it will mark the beginning of the Tribulation (as a false treaty). She has listened to many end-time preachers and is convinced that "Christians" will go thru the Tribulation period, or at least the first three-and-one-half years. Anyway, I told her that we believe 1 Thessalonians 4:15-18: *"Then we which are alive and remain shall be caught up together with them in the clouds to meet the Lord in the air."*

You mention in your teaching and preaching God's Words in your Revelation book about Daniel 9:24: *"Seventy weeks are determined upon thy people."* Does this word "people" mean lost? Because you go on to say, "That is why you don't believe the true church has any part of the Tribulation."

When did the last week of Daniel's 70th week begin? and when "possibly" does it play out? 5-10 years? 10-20 years? I'm not sure I understand. Does 1 week equal one year? What is your best guess?
ANSWER #1373
I'm sorry for your friend who believes saved people will go through at least half of the Tribulation. She's been taught wrong and probably nothing will convince her otherwise. You are correct on the

pre-Tribulation Rapture of saved people to meet the Lord Jesus Christ in the air.

The clear teaching of Daniel 9:24 is that the Tribulation is for "*thy people*," meaning for Israel. It is not for the church to go through. The Tribulation's seven years is called elsewhere as Daniel's 70th week because this verse says that "*seventy years*" are determined in Israel. This is 70 weeks of years or 70 7's or a total of 490 years. 69 weeks or 483 years have already been fulfilled on Israel, and this leaves only one more week of 7 years that is left to complete God's dealings with His people Israel.

We do not know exactly when this last week of 7 years begins. We do know that it will begin at the Rapture of all the genuine Christians and will extend for 7 years after which the Lord Jesus Christ will come back to this earth and set up His thousand year millennial reign.

Burgon's Church Fathers Index
QUESTION #1374
I noted from something that you've published that Dean Burgon had an unrealized project to make known to the world the Church Fathers' use of the Traditional Text. Apparently he compiled an index of over 86,000 quotations to demonstrate his point. Could you please tell me whether or not this work has ever been published? Is anyone working on getting this material out to the people of God? If not, do you think it a worthwhile venture to make this happen?
ANSWER #1374
Burgon's index of over 86,000 quotations of the Bible by the church fathers is available in London, England, in the form in which Dean Burgon wrote it. I asked Dr. Jack Moorman, one of our church's missionaries in London, many years ago, to check out the possibilities of re-printing this index. He looked into it and had a number of things to say about this project: (1) The work is in color to highlight various things; (2) To reprint in color would be extremely expensive; (3) The library, where the work is, charges quite a bit per page even to make copies of it; (4) We would need to have the exact edition of each of the church fathers that Burgon had, in order to come up with the right page of the quotation; (5) In conclusion, it does not look like this project is probable.

Dr. Moorman has a section in his book *EARLY MANUSCRIPTS, CHURCH FATHERS, AND THE AUTHORIZED VERSION* **(BFT #3230 @ $25.00 +$10.00 S&H)** on the church fathers which sums up their testimony to the New Testament. It is on pages

313-432 of that book. You might order that book to see this summation.

Status Of Saved Jews

QUESTION #1375

The Church will be with Christ in the New Jerusalem. The Church will be made up of former Jews and Gentiles that are genuinely saved since the Church was formed at Pentecost. Now, who are the Jews who will be in the Kingdom during the Millennium? Will they be the Jews saved during the Tribulation–the Tribulation saints?

ANSWER #1375

The answer to your questions is not crystal clear in the Bible, but here is one possibility:

1.   You are right that the true Church will be made up of former Jews and Gentiles that are genuinely saved from the day of Pentecost until the Rapture.

2.   I believe that the Jews in the Kingdom during the Millennium will be those saved during the Tribulation and possibly the saved Jews from Abraham to the end of Malachi and the Tribulation saints. This is not clear, however.

3.   The "Israel of God" it seems, in Galatians 6:16, refers to those who are genuinely saved in the age of grace, whether former Jews or former Gentiles.

These answers are not made crystal clear in the Bible and so they must be surmises and guesses only.

Erasmus Commentaries

QUESTION #1376

Do you know anything about the Erasmus Commentaries? Do you think they are reliable?

ANSWER #1376

I heard about Erasmus' commentaries the other day, though I have not read them. Even though he stood for the Received Greek Text, he was a Roman Catholic priest. As such, I would assume that he believed many of the heretical teachings of that church. As such, I wouldn't trust his opinions on the doctrines of the Bible.

The Tribulation

QUESTION #1377

There is a question I have on 1 Thessalonians 4:18. It is mentioned that the first 3 ½ years will be peaceful. What kind of peace is that referring to?

ANSWER #1377

1   Thessalonians   4:18   *"Wherefore* **comfort** *one another with these words."*

The "*comfort*" in 1 Thessalonians 4:18 has to do with the genuine Christians who are living at the time of the Pre-Tribulation Rapture of all true Christians by the Lord Jesus Christ. These Christians will be comforted in knowing that their fellow Christians who died before the Rapture will take part in the Rapture and will be re-united with the living Christians. This is the reason for the "*comfort*."

This Rapture will take place before any part of the seven-year Tribulation begins. During the seven years that follow the Rapture of the saved, there will be a relative peaceful 3 ½ years when the Antichrist seems like a good person who will promise man things which are simply lies. The Antichrist's true character will be shown during the last 3½ years of the Tribulation. He will behead, imprison, and murder thousands and thousands on the earth. I think these murders and slaughters belong to the last 3 ½ years of the Tribulation.

How Can Heathen Be Saved?

QUESTION #1378

How can a person who lives in the Amazon jungle who has never heard of the Lord Jesus Christ be saved?

ANSWER #1378

The clear answer from God's **special revelation** in the Bible on being saved is that a person must genuinely receive the Lord Jesus Christ as their Saviour by personal faith.

The unclear answer from God's **general revelation** in His creation is if they somehow heed God's "*invisible things of Him from the creation f the world,*" God might graciously receive them as He did before the Lord Jesus Christ came into the world and died for the sins of the world. The unclear answer is just that--unclear. It is in God's hands. We must keep using God's clear answer in every way possible, and leave the unclear answer to the Lord Himself.

Romans 1:19-20

"Because that which may be known of God is manifest in them; for God hath shewed it unto them. 20 ***For the invisible things of him from the creation of the world are clearly seen, being understood by the things that are made, even his eternal power and Godhead****; so that they are without excuse:"*

Where Is Mount Pisgah?
QUESTION #1379
Could you tell me where Mount Pisgah is today (modern land)?
ANSWER #1379
According to one article
(http://en.wikipedia.org/wiki/Mount_Pisgah_%28Bible%29)
> *"The region is directly east of the Jordan River and just northeast of the Dead Sea. Mount Nebo (31°45.9'N 35°43.1'E) is the highest among a handful of Pisgah summits; an arid cluster of hilltops on the western edge of the Trans-Jordanian Plateau."*

So if you can find the Jordan and look east, and then find the Dead Sea and go just a little northeast of that, there is Mount Pisgah.

Hamas vs. Israel
QUESTION #1380
What do you think of this old Jewish man's short speech?
http://youtu.be/qMGuYjt6CP8
UK Jewish MP speaks in the House of Commons--5 minutes long
ANSWER #1380
I listened to the 5-minute speaker. From what he said, he was friends with one of the former Hamas leaders. He thinks Hamas, since it was elected by the people, is *"the only game in town"* and should be followed. This is an error. Israel is fighting for its life and its land. Hamas has sent thousands of rockets over into Israel to ruin it. They have made tunnels into Israel to allow bombers to blow themselves up and kill many Israeli people. It is not Israel that is acting like Nazis; it is Hamas, and all the ISIS butchers that are operating all around the Middle East. That's my take on this. I support the Israeli Prime Minister in his defense of his land and his people.

Strong's Or Young's Concordances
QUESTION #1381
I have *Young's Concordance*. I believe it is a better one than Strong's. Is this true?
ANSWER #1381
I have both Young's and Strong's. Both have good features. I like Strong's best because it follows the English words alphabetically from Genesis through Revelation consecutively. Young's gives you

the Hebrew or Greek word and the English that go with those words rather than going right through the Bible on the one English word you're looking for.

Geocentricity vs. Heliocentricity
QUESTION #1382

Job 26:7   *"He stretcheth out the north over the empty place, and **hangeth the earth upon nothing**."*

When the Bible says that the Earth hangs on nothing, does that imply stationariness or motion?

ANSWER #1382

I believe the earth hanging on nothing implies stationariness, rather than motion.   Dr. Jack Moorman's excellent book on *"GEOCENTRICITY, THE BIBLICAL AND OBSERVATIONAL CASE"* **(BFT #4054 @ $20.00 + $8.00 S&H)** gives almost 100 Bible references to the stable and stationary earth. This view used to be held by both followers of the Bible and science. Then science departed to a heliocentric view where the sun was the center of the universe rather than the earth. It is a very complicated subject, but Dr. Moorman does an excellent job in using the Bible to prove geocentricity.

Bible Dictionaries
QUESTION #1383

I have been trying to find a "good" Bible dictionary. The ones I have seem to have some contradictions. In some places the wording seems that the authors must not have been true Christians. What is a good dependable Bible dictionary?

ANSWER #1383

You will always find things you might not agree with in various Bible dictionaries. Most of them do not use the King James Bible, for example. I guess you have to take the things that are accurate in such Bible dictionaries, and reject the things that are contradictory. *Unger's Bible Dictionary* is one with such things you might agree with as well as things you might disagree with. You must have discernment as you read these Bible dictionaries.

Tribulation And Losing Salvation
QUESTION #1384

Are the people who believe they can lose their salvation the very same people who believe they are going to go through the Tribulation?

ANSWER #1384

These who hold to this unBiblical position of being able to lose their genuine salvation might either believe or not believe in such a time as the Tribulation. They also might believe or not believe in the pre-Tribulation Rapture of true Christians. I don't think a statement can be made about tying these two false views together. I'm not denying that there might be some who believe them both. On the other hand, some might believe one, but not the other.

The Book Of Life

QUESTION #1385

I need to know, if there is Scripture to say when a person's name is written in the book of life. Is it when we are born, before we are born, or when we are born-again?

ANSWER #1385

It is somewhat difficult to answer this, since there different ways this expression is used in both the Old and the New Testaments. Below are all the verses where *"the book of life"* expression is found. Here is a verse which has *"my book."*

> **Exodus 32:33** *"And the LORD said unto Moses, Whosoever hath sinned against me, him will I blot out of **my book**."*

Your question has been answered in different ways. The preceding verse seems to indicate that, in the Old Testament age of the law of Moses, all the Israelites were in God's book, until they sinned against Him. Then they would be blotted out. That seems to be a reasonable explanation that answers your question as far as the Old Testament teachings.

Look at the New Testament verses that mention **"the book of life"** to see what the teaching is now. From looking at all these verses, it is not clear about the answer to your question. One thing seems to be clear, however. Only those whose names are in ***"the book of life"*** will go to Heaven.

> **Philippians 4:3** *"And I intreat thee also, true yokefellow, help those women which laboured with me in the gospel, with Clement also, and with other my fellowlabourers, whose names are in **the book of life**."*

> **Revelation 3:5** *"He that overcometh, the same shall be clothed in white raiment; and I will not blot out his name out of **the book of life**, but I will confess his name before my Father, and before his angels."*

Revelation 13:8 *"And all that dwell upon the earth shall worship him, whose names are not written in* **the book of life** *of the Lamb slain from the foundation of the world."*

Revelation 17:8 *"The beast that thou sawest was, and is not; and shall ascend out of the bottomless pit, and go into perdition: and they that dwell on the earth shall wonder, whose names were not written in* **the book of life** *from the foundation of the world, when they behold the beast that was, and is not, and yet is.:*

Revelation 20:15 *"And whosoever was not found written in* **the book of life** *was cast into the lake of fire."*

Revelation 21:27 *"And there shall in no wise enter into it any thing that defileth, neither whatsoever worketh abomination, or maketh a lie: but they which are written in* **the Lamb's book of life**.*"*

Revelation 22:19 "And if any man shall take away from the words of the book of this prophecy, God shall take away his part out of **the book of life**, and out of the holy city, and from the things which are written in this book."

Who Saved In The Tribulation

QUESTION #1386

2 Thessalonians 2:9 *"Even him, whose coming is after the working of Satan* **with all power and signs and lying wonders**,*"*

2 Thessalonians 2:10 *"**And with all deceivableness of unrighteousness in them that perish; because they received not the love of the truth, that they might be saved**."*

2 Thessalonians 2:11 *"And for this cause* **God shall send them strong delusion, that they should believe a lie**:*"*

2 Thessalonians 2:12 *"**That they all might be damned who believed not the truth**, but had pleasure in unrighteousness."*

There is one aspect of Thessalonians which I wonder about. I just find myself not really agreeing with the teaching on 2 Thessalonians 2:9-12. Here is some of my reasoning, which perhaps I'm wrong in it but thought I'd send it along. I don't think that those who have heard the gospel message before the Tribulation have no opportunity to turn to the Lord during that time to be saved. Is this position wrong?

ANSWER #1386

There are some who take your position, but the section that I, and many others use, is in connection with these verses. The Antichrist and Satan will deceive those in the Tribulation and send them "***strong delusion, that they should believe a lie.***" They will not receive the Lord Jesus Christ as their Saviour. But "*they all might be damned who believed not the truth.*" These are the verses that I, and many others who believe as I do, rest upon.

You and others can take a different interpretation on these verses if you wish, of course. What do the verses mean if they don't mean that these Tribulation people will "**believe a lie**" and "**be damned who believed not the truth**"?

Strong Delusion In Tribulation
QUESTION #1387

Are you saying that only those who have heard the gospel message prior to the Tribulation will have the strong delusion sent to them? Are you saying that those who have not heard the gospel message prior to the Tribulation and who are rejecting it during the Tribulation when they hear it at first--that they could still be saved later at various times during the Tribulation?

ANSWER #1387

I believe that the Jews who are saved by the ministry of the 144,000 Jewish evangelists were Jews who never heard the gospel of Christ before then. They will receive the Lord Jesus Christ as their Saviour and not take the mark of the beast. Only those who have heard and rejected the gospel message prior to the Tribulation will have the "*strong delusion*" sent to them and that those who have not heard the gospel message prior to the Tribulation who are rejecting it during the Tribulation when they hear it at first that they could still be saved later at various times during the Tribulation (like the Jewish remnant).

Speaking In Tongues Today

QUESTION #1388

1 Corinthians 13:8   *"Charity never faileth: but whether there be prophecies, they shall fail; whether there be **tongues, they shall cease**; whether there be knowledge, it shall vanish away."*

1 Corinthians 13:9 *"For we know in part, and we prophesy in part."*

1 Corinthians 13:10   *"But **when that which is perfect is come**, then that which is in part shall be done away."*

1 Corinthians 13:11 *"When I was a child, I spake as a child, I understood as a child, I thought as a child: but when I became a man, I put away childish things."*

I went to a church service where someone spoke in tongues and then another person interpreted. Could you please explain this for me? How do we know this is ever of God?

ANSWER #1388

Let me say a few things about tongues for the present times:

1.   In Acts 2, they were clearly foreign languages that God used to evangelize the many nations that gathered together in Jerusalem at the feast of Pentecost.

2.   In 1 Corinthians 14, there was an order of speaking and interpreting during the apostolic years.

3.   The verses above teach that "*tongues, they shall cease*" along with the two other things mentioned.

4.   When did this take place? This gift of speaking and interpreting these foreign languages was to end "**when that which is perfect is come**." "**That which is perfect**" is a Greek neuter gender noun, (TO TELEION). It is not a Greek masculine gender noun. It therefore could not refer to the coming again of the Lord Jesus Christ as some interpret it. Being a Greek neuter in gender, it must refer to a neuter gender Greek noun. I believe it refers to TO BIBLION ("the Bible"). It would then mean when the Bible has been completed, then all these temporary gifts will "*fail*," "*cease*," and "*vanish away*." The Bible was completed in 90 or 100 A.D. From then on, all these temporary gifts given by God have been eliminated. I believe that the so-called gifts practiced today by the Pentecostals and Charismatics are phony, false, apostate, and unBiblical.

The Bride Of Christ
QUESTION #1389

I never knew that there was an issue concerning who the Bride of Christ is. Could you take a moment and explain this for me?

ANSWER #1389

In the Ephesians verses below, it is implied that genuine Christians have the Lord Jesus Christ as their Heavenly Husband, making them His "*bride*." In some of the Revelation verses, the term, "*bride*" is used of those who are true Christians in Heaven. I believe that the term, the "*bride of Christ*" would refer to those who are genuine Christians from the Day of Pentecost until they are taken to Heaven in the Rapture of Christ.

Ephesians 5:23 "*For the husband is the head of the wife, even as Christ is the head of the church: and he is the saviour of the body.*"

Ephesians 5:24 "*Therefore as the church is subject unto Christ, so let the wives be to their own husbands in every thing.*"

Ephesians 5:25 "*Husbands, love your wives, even as Christ also loved the church, and gave himself for it;*"

John 3:29 "**_He that hath the bride is the bridegroom_**: *but the friend of the bridegroom, which standeth and heareth him, rejoiceth greatly because of the bridegroom's voice: this my joy therefore is fulfilled.*"

Revelation 18:23 "*And the light of a candle shall shine no more at all in thee; and **the voice of the bridegroom and of the bride shall be heard no more at all in thee: for thy** merchants were the great men of the earth; for by thy sorceries were all nations deceived.*"

Revelation 21:2 "*And I John saw the holy city, new Jerusalem, coming down from God out of heaven, **prepared as a bride adorned for her husband**.*"

Revelation 21:9 "*And there came unto me one of the seven angels which had the seven vials full of the seven last plagues, and talked with me, saying, Come hither, **I will shew thee the bride**, the Lamb's wife.*"

> Revelation 22:17 *"And **the Spirit and the bride say, Come**. And let him that heareth say, Come. And let him that is athirst come. And whosoever will, let him take the water of life freely."*

The Bride Of Christ #2
QUESTION #1390
Would it be correct to refer to the bride of Christ in all three of these meanings below?

1.   Genuine Christians have the Lord Jesus Christ as their Heavenly Husband
2.   Those who are true Christians in Heaven
3.   Those who are truly saved from the Day of Pentecost until they are taken to Heaven in the Rapture of Christ

ANSWER #1390
I believe that all three of your definitions could be included as the "bride of Christ."

Salvation Terms Calvinist?
QUESTION #1391
I have a friend who writes a newsletter for a small ministry. She's written this: *"We understand that only the Holy Spirit can convert a person to the saving knowledge of Jesus Christ."* Does this sound Calvinist to you?

ANSWER #1391
While it is true that God the Holy Spirit witnesses to lost people, this is not one-sided in isolation of the person's own personal faith in the Lord Jesus Christ.   John 3:16 (below) is very clear that *"everlasting life"* is for *"whosoever believeth"* in the Lord Jesus Christ.   If personal faith is omitted, Bible salvation cannot be accomplished. In Ephesians 2:8 (below) without a person's genuine *"faith"* they cannot be saved.

> John 3:16 *"For God so loved the world, that he gave his only begotten Son, that whosoever believeth in him should not perish, but have everlasting life."*

> Ephesians 2:8 *"For **by grace are ye saved through faith**; and that not of yourselves: it is the gift of God:"*

A Holy Spirit Song
QUESTION #1392

I may be doing this song and want to interpret the lyrics the right way. I put in bold lettering with an underline the lyrics my question is about. Should I sing "His blessed Holy Spirit" or "The blessed Holy Spirit" or does it make a difference?

"LEARNING TO LEAN"
Writer John Stallings
The joy I can't explain fills my heart,
Since the day I made Jesus my King;
<u>His blessed Holy Spirit</u> *is leading my way,*
He's teaching and I'm learning to lean.
Chorus
I'm learning to lean, learning to lean,
Learning to lean on Jesus.
Finding more power than I'd ever dreamed,
I'm learning to lean on Jesus.

ANSWER #1392

I think "*the blessed Holy Spirit*" would be better. If you say "*His Blessed Holy Spirit*" it would imply that the Lord Jesus Christ is the originator or the owner of God the Holy Spirit. This is not true. God the Holy Spirit is a separate, equal, and omnipotent member of the Triune God--God the Father, God the Son, and God the Holy Spirit.

Separating From Hyper-Calvinism
QUESTION #1393

I have a group of friends who are studying the subject of Eternal Security from Arnold Fruchtenbaum, a respected Messianic Jew, a Calvinist, and a graduate of DTS. I had hoped to join them, but when I reviewed the manuscript, I saw that he predicates eternal security on sovereign election, mentions the sovereign purposes of God in several places; he changed the word "*foreknew*" to "*foreordain*" in Romans 8:28, and he mentions election. I won't be attending this study because of the Calvinism, but I'm a bit depressed that these friends aren't taking a stand against this study, after all they've learned about Calvinism. And if they won't separate, what does that say for the majority of Christendom? Would you let me know if me staying out is the right thing to do, just for my own benefit? I feel that it is, but I'm trying to strike the right balance between loving people and separating from error.

ANSWER #1393

Thanks for your note about the DTS graduate of recent years (more recent than when I graduated from there in 1952 and 1954) and his hyper-Calvinism. I think your discernment about his equating his view of eternal security with Calvinistic-election is a heretical view which blocks out all the many proofs for eternal security from Biblical truth. This could mean that he would be neglecting the many other proofs because of his election blindness. As the verse below mentions, it appears that this Calvinist election teacher is disorderly and not after the "*tradition*" that Paul and others teach about concerning eternal security. You did right in not attending this class and thus seeming to agree with his errors.

> **2 Thessalonians 3:6**   "*Now we command you, brethren, in the name of our Lord Jesus Christ, that ye withdraw yourselves from every brother that walketh disorderly, and not after the tradition which he received of us.*"

Dynamic Equivalent Translations

QUESTION #1394

Kindly advise the type and cost of the documents you have available to show that the ESV, NASB and NET are dynamic equivalencies, not literal-translation Bibles.

ANSWER #1394

We have several thousand titles we carry defending the Traditional Hebrew, Aramaic, and Greek Words. I discuss the errors of dynamic equivalent translations in many of these. I'll list a few that answer your questions the best:

1.   My book *DEFENDING THE KING JAMES BIBLE* (**BFT #1594 @ $12.00 + $6.00 S&H**)

2.   Dr. Jack Moorman's books

a.   *8,000 DIFFERENCES BETWEEN THE CRITICAL TEXT AND THE T.R.* (**BFT #3084 @ $20.00 + $10.00 S&H**)

b.   *EARLY MANUSCRIPTS, CHURCH FATHERS & THE AUTHORIZED VERSION* (**BFT #3230 @20.00 + $10.00 S&H**) He shows about 200 pages of 356 theological passages where all three of these translations are in theological error.

3.   My book, *THE NASV ANALYZED--4,000 Additions, Subtractions or other changes from the original Words* (**BFT #1494 @ $15.00 + $8.00 S&H**)

4.   *THE ENGLISH STANDARD VERSION DEFICIENCIES, SEVERAL ARTICLES BY SEVERAL WRITERS* (**BFT #4106 @ $7.00 + $4.00 S&H**)

Steven Anderson's False Beliefs

QUESTION #1395

What are the beliefs of Steven Anderson? Is he sound?

ANSWER #1395

He is not sound in many areas. The link below gives some of the Doctrinal Beliefs of Steven Anderson of the Faithful Word Baptist Church in Tempe, Arizona. Here are some of the Biblical errors believed by Steven Anderson:

1.   He wrongly believes that the King James Bible is *"inspired"* or *"God-Breathed"* rather than being a skilled and an accurate translation of the inspired, God-breathed, and preserved original Hebrew, Aramaic, and Greek Words.

2.   He denies the *"church which is His body"* (Ephesians 1:22-23) including every genuine Christian from the day of Pentecost until the Rapture by the Lord Jesus Christ of every true Christian. He believes only in local churches.

3.   He wrongly believes in the Post-Tribulation Rapture of the true Christians rather than the Biblical Pre-Tribulation Rapture. He believes genuine Christians must go through the seven-year Tribulation.

http://www.faithfulwordbaptist.org/page6.html

Good Christian Music

QUESTION #1396

I need advice on what is good Christian music. Out of CCM I very rarely find something that I can call acceptable. The same goes for most of the Southern Gospel or bluegrass Gospel. I have found some bluegrass Gospel that I find okay, but still have to be cautious. What are some examples of good Christian music? I have a ministry of music. I play harmonica and sing. But I want to make sure I am playing the right music. Can you help guide me in this area?

ANSWER #1396

I believe you can't go wrong with the traditional hymns and gospel songs of former days. There are some all right in these days, but I don't trust them either because of the jazz rhythm, or who the writer is, or some other things. We use the *Majesty Hymn Book*, but many of these hymns we cannot sing for various reasons. We do sing the traditional hymns that are found that that hymn book. Here are some of them: (1) A Mighty Fortress; (2) A Shelter in the Time of Storm; (3) All the Way My Saviour Leads Me; (4) Amazing Grace; (5) At Calvary; (6) At The Cross; (7) Be Still My Soul; (8) Beneath the Cross of Jesus; (9) Be Thou Exalted; (10) Blessed Assurance; (11)

Blessed Redeemer; (12) Channels Only; (13) Christ Arose, and many, many more.

Altar Calls
QUESTION #1397
My question is when leading someone to Christ as their Saviour, do you have to have an altar call? Is Romans 10:9 telling us to make an open and public confession, or is it more of a personal recognition that Jesus is Lord?

Romans 10:9 *"That if thou shalt **confess with thy mouth the Lord Jesus**, and shalt believe in thine heart that God hath raised him from the dead, thou shalt be saved."*

ANSWER #1397
In leading someone to a saving knowledge of the Lord Jesus Christ, you do not need to have an altar call. This can be done person to person and need not be done in a church service. After a person becomes a genuine Christian and is born-again, they should confess the Lord Jesus Christ to others and be a good witness in every area of their life. This does not limit their witness to a church meeting.

Dr. Strouse And The KJBRC Group
QUESTION #1398
Before I close I have one question–Is there any update on what Dr. Strouse and the KJBRC (King James Bible Research Council) is doing? I fear that the effects of this are spreading.

ANSWER #1398
I haven't heard from Dr. Strouse for a while. He is no longer with the Dean Burgon Society, but still stands for the KJB and its underlying Hebrew, Aramaic, and Greek Words. However, he denies "the church which is His body" (Ephesians 1:22-23), but insists that his kind of local Baptist Churches are the only *"body of Christ."* All sound others are only in the *"family of God."*

I suppose the KJBRC is doing the same as always. Their doctrinal statement is quite defective. I have a PDF that explains 14 serious doctrinal omissions from their doctrinal statement. This is available for those who request it.

Who Is Lucifer?

QUESTION #1399

A friend of mine forwarded this to me from some web page about Lucifer. Who is he?

ANSWER #1399

The context of these verses below from Isaiah 14:12-15 alludes to Satan's five "*I wills.*" It doesn't refer to anyone else. The word Lucifer comes from two Latin words, LUX ("*light*") and FERO ("*to bear or to carry*"). He is an angel of light (2 Corinthians 11:14 "*And no marvel; for Satan himself is transformed into an angel of light.*")

The Hebrew Word translated "*Lucifer*" is HELEL. This means "*light bearer, or shining one.*" Lucifer is an excellent translation of the Hebrew Word HELEL. It has nothing whatsoever to do with "*evening star*" or "*morning star.*" This is a false translation of the term. There is no Hebrew Word for either "*morning*" or "*evening*" or for "*star.*"

> **Isaiah 14:12** "*How art thou fallen from heaven, O Lucifer, son of the morning! how art thou cut down to the ground, which didst weaken the nations!*"
>
> **Isaiah 14:13** "*For thou hast said in thine heart, I will ascend into heaven, I will exalt my throne above the stars of God: I will sit also upon the mount of the congregation, in the sides of the north:*"
>
> **Isaiah 14:14** "*I will ascend above the heights of the clouds; I will be like the most High.*"
>
> **Isaiah 14:15** "*Yet thou shalt be brought down to hell, to the sides of the pit.*"

Meaning of "Pastors"

QUESTION #1400

Can you give me a greater understanding of what the term "*pastors*" means that is used here by Jeremiah?

> **Jeremiah 3:15** "*And I will give you pastors according to mine heart, which shall feed you with knowledge and understanding.*"

ANSWER #1400

I have included a lengthy article to you on the meaning of the Hebrew word RAAH. In summary, it means to act like a shepherd to people in the Old Testament. The Greek Word, POIMENOS, for "*pastor*" also means to act like a shepherd to people, helping them and leading them.

Index Of Words And Phrases

About The Author

The author of this book, Dr. D. A. Waite, received a BA (Bachelor of Arts) in classical Greek and Latin from the University of Michigan in 1948, a ThM (Master of Theology), with high honors, in New Testament Greek Literature and Exegesis from Dallas Theological Seminary in 1952, an MA (Master of Arts) in Speech from Southern Methodist University in 1953, a ThD (Doctor of Theology), with honors, in Bible Exposition from Dallas Theological Seminary in 1955, and a PhD in Speech from Purdue University in 1961. He held both New Jersey and Pennsylvania teacher certificates in Greek and Language Arts.

He has been a teacher in the areas of Greek, Hebrew, Bible, Speech, and English for over thirty-five years in ten schools, including one junior high, one senior high, four Bible institutes, two colleges, two universities, and one seminary. He served his country as a Navy Chaplain for five years on active duty; pastored three churches; was Chairman and Director of the Radio and Audio-Film Commission of the American Council of Christian Churches; since 1969, has been Founder, President, and Director of THE BIBLE FOR TODAY; since 1978, has been Founder and President of the DEAN BURGON SOCIETY; has produced over 700 other studies, books, cassettes, VHS's, CD's, or VCR's on various topics IN DEFENSE OF TRADITIONAL BIBLE TEXTS, on radio, shortwave, and streaming on the Internet at BibleForToday.org, 24/7/365 on the BROWN BOX.

Dr. and Mrs. Waite have been married since 1948; they have four sons, one daughter, and, at present, eight grandchildren, and fifteen great-grandchildren. Since October 4, 1998, he has been the Pastor of the Bible For Today Baptist Church in Collingswood, New Jersey. His sermons are heard both on radio and the Internet over www.BibleForToday.org on the BROWN BOX.

Order Blank (p. 1)

Name:_____

Address:_____

City & State:_____Zip:_____

Credit Card #:_____Expires:_____

Verse by Verse Preaching Books by Dr. D. A. Waite

[ ] Send 2 Peter & Jude–Preaching Verse B Verse by Pastor D. A. Waite, 215 pages ($15.00 + $8.00 @ S&H) fully indexed.

[ ] Send *1 & 2 Thessalonians–Preaching Verse by Verse* by Pastor D. A. Waite, 327 pages ($15.00 + $8.00 S&H) fully indexed.

[ ] Send *Hebrews–Preaching Verse by Verse*, by Pastor D. A. Waite, 616 pages ($30.00 +$10.00 S&H) fully indexed.

[ ] Send *Revelation–Preaching Verse by Verse*, by Pastor D. A. Waite, 1032 pages ($50.00 + $10.00 S&H) fully indexed.

[ ] Send *1 Timothy--Preaching Verse by Verse*, by Pastor D. A. Waite, 288 pages, hardback ($11+$5 S&H) fully indexed.

[ ] Send *2 Timothy--Preaching Verse by Verse*, by Pastor D. A. Waite, 250 pages, hardback ($11+$5 S&H) fully indexed.

[ ] Send *Romans--Preaching Verse by Verse* by Pastor D. A. Waite 736 pp. Hardback ($25+$8 S&H) fully indexed

[ ] Send *Colossians & Philemon--Preaching Verse by Verse* by Pastor D. A. Waite ($12+$5 S&H) hardback, 240 pages.

[ ] Send *Philippians--Preaching Verse by Verse* by Pastor D. A. Waite ($10+$5 S&H) hardback, 176 pages. fully indexed.

[ ] Send *Ephesians--Preaching Verse by Verse* by Pastor D. A. Waite ($12+$5 S&H) hardback, 224 pages. fully indexed.

[ ] Send *Galatians--Preaching Verse By Verse* by Pastor D. A. Waite ($12+$5 S&H) hardback, 216 pages. fully indexed.

[ ] Send *1 Peter–Preaching Verse By Verse* by Pastor D. A. Waite ($10.00 + $5.00 S&H) hardback, 176 pages. fully indexed.

Other Books by Dr. D. A. Waite

[ ] Send *A Critical Answer to God's Word Preserved* by Pastor D. A. Waite, 192 pp. perfect bound ($11.00+$4.00 S&H)

Send or Call Orders to:
THE BIBLE FOR TODAY
900 Park Ave., Collingswood, NJ 08108
Phone: 856-854-4452; FAX:--2464; Orders: 1-800 JOHN 10:9
E-Mail Orders: BFT@BibleForToday.org; Credit Cards OK

Order Blank (p. 3)

Name:_____

Address:_____

City & State:_____Zip:_____

Credit Card #:_____Expires:_____

[ ] Send *Making Marriage Melodious* by Pastor D. A. Waite ($7+$4 S&H), perfect bound, 112 pages.

[ ] Send *Burgon's Warnings on Revision* by DAW ($7+$4 S&H) A perfect bound book, 120 pages in length.

[ ] Send *The Superior Foundation of the KJB* by Dr. D. A. Waite ($10.00 + $7.00 S&H)

Other Books by Dr. D. A. Waite (Continued)

[ ] Send *Biblical Separation–1,896 Bible Verses About It* by Dr. D. A. Waite ($14.00 + $7.00 S&H)

[ ] Send *Westcott & Hort's Greek Text & Theory Refuted by Burgon's Revision Revised--Summarized* by Dr. D. A. Waite ($7.00+$4 S&H), 120 pages, perfect bound.

[ ] Send *Dean Burgon's Confidence in KJB* by DAW ($3+$3)

[ ] Send *Vindicating Mark 16:9-20* by Dr. Waite ($3+$3S&H)

[ ] Send *Summary of Traditional Text* by Dr. Waite ($3 +$3)

[ ] Send *Summary of Causes of Corruption*, DAW ($3+$3)

[ ] Send *Summary of Inspiration* by Dr. Waite ($3+$3 S&H)

[ ] Send *Soulwinning's Versions-Perversions* by Dr. D. A. Waite ($6.00 + $5.00 S&H)

Books by Dean John William Burgon

[ ] Send *The Revision Revised* by Dean Burgon ($25 + $5 S&H) A hardback book, 640 pages in length.

[ ] Send *The Last 12 verses of Mark* by Dean Burgon ($15+$5 S&H) A hardback book 400 pages.

[ ] Send *The Traditional Text* hardback by Burgon ($16+$5 S&H) A hardback book, 384 pages in length.

[ ] Send *Causes of Corruption* by Burgon ($15+$5 S&H) A hardback book, 360 pages in length.

Send or Call Orders to:
THE BIBLE FOR TODAY
900 Park Ave., Collingswood, NJ 08108
Phone: 856-854-4452; FAX:--2464; Orders: 1-800 JOHN 10:9
E-Mail Orders: BFT@BibleForToday.org; Credit Cards OK

Order Blank (p. 4)

Name:_____

Address:_____

City & State:_____Zip:_____

Credit Card #:_____Expires:_____

[ ] Send *Inspiration and Interpretation*, Dean Burgon ($25+$5 S&H) A hardback book, 610 pages in length.

Books by Dr. Jack Moorman

[ ] Send *Samuel P. Tregelles--The Man Who Made the Critical Text Acceptable to Bible Believers* by Dr. Moorman ($2+$1)

[ ] Send *8,000 Differences Between TR & CT* by Dr. Jack Moorman [$65 + $7.50 S&H] Over 500-large-pages of data

[ ] Send *356 Doctrinal Errors in the NIV & Other Modern Versions*, 100-large-pages, $10.00+$6 S&H.

[ ] Send *The Doctrinal Heart of the Bible--Removed from Modern Versions* by Dr. Jack Moorman, VCR, $15 +$4 S&H

[ ] Send *Modern Bibles--The Dark Secret* by Dr. Jack Moorman, $5+$3 S&H

[ ] Send *The Manuscript Digest of the N.T.* (721 pp.) by Dr. Jack Moorman, copy-machine bound ($50+$7 S&H)

[ ] *Early Manuscripts, Church Fathers, & the Authorized Version* by Dr. Jack Moorman, $18+$5 S&H. Hardback

[ ] Send *Forever Settled--Bible Documents & History Survey* by Dr. Jack Moorman, $20+$5 S&H. Hardback book.

[ ] Send *When the KJB Departs from the So-Called "Majority Text"* by Dr. Jack Moorman, $16+$5 S&H

[ ] Send *Missing in Modern Bibles--Nestle-Aland/NIV Errors* by Dr. Jack Moorman, $8+$4 S&H

Books by Miscellaneous Authors

[ ] Send *Guide to Textual Criticism* by Edward Miller ($7+$4) Hardback book

[ ] Send *Scrivener's Greek New Testament Underlying the King James Bible*, hardback, ($14+$5 S&H)

Send or Call Orders to:
THE BIBLE FOR TODAY
900 Park Ave., Collingswood, NJ 08108
Phone: 856-854-4452; FAX:--2464; Orders: 1-800 JOHN 10:9
E-Mail Orders: BFT@BibleForToday.org; Credit Cards OK

Order Blank (p. 5)

Name:_____

Address:_____

City & State:_____ Zip:_____

Credit Card #:_____ Expires:_____

[ ] Send *Scrivener's Annotated Greek New Testament,* by Dr. Frederick Scrivener: Hardback--($35+$5 S&H); Genuine Leather--($45+$5 S&H)

[ ] Send *Why Not the King James Bible?--An Answer to James White's KJVO Book* by Dr. K. D. DiVietro, $10+$5 S&H

[ ] Send Brochure #1: *"1000 Titles Defending the KJB/TR"* No Charge

[ ] Send *The LIE That Changed the Modern World* by Dr. H. D. Williams ($16+$5 S&H) Hardback book

[ ] Send *With Tears in My Heart* by Gertrude G. Sanborn. Hardback 414 pp. ($25+$5 S&H) 400 Christian Poems

[ ] Send *Dean Burgon's Defense of the Authorised Version* by Dr. David Bennett ($14.0 + 8.00 S&H)

[ ] Send *Drift in Baptist Missions, Churches & Schools* by Dr. David Bennett ($12.00 + $8.00 S&H)

More Books by Miscellaneous Authors

[ ] Send *Able To Bear It* by Gertrude Sanborn ($14.00 + $7.00 S&H

[ ] Send *Visitation In Action* by Mr. R. O. Sanborn ($10.00 + $7.00 S&H)

[ ] Send *Daily Bible Blessings From Daily Bible Readings* by Yvonne Sanborn Waite ($30.00 + $10.00 S&H)

[ ] Send *Husband-Loving Lessons* by Yvonne Sanborn Waite ($25.00 + $8.00 S&H)

[ ] Send *Gnosticism--The Doctrinal Foundation of New Bibles* by J. Moser ($20.00 + $8.00 S&H)

Send or Call Orders to:
THE BIBLE FOR TODAY
900 Park Ave., Collingswood, NJ 08108
Phone: 856-854-4452; FAX:--2464; Orders: 1-800 JOHN 10:9
E-Mail Orders: BFT@BibleForToday.org; Credit Cards OK

Order Blank (p. 6)

Name:_____

Address:_____

City & State:_____Zip:_____

Credit Card #:_____Expires:_____

[ ] Send *God's Marvelous Book* by Dr. David Bennett ($15.00 + $8.00 S&H)

[ ] Send *CCM Not The Problem–Only A Symptom* by Dr. David Bennett ($12.00 + $7.00 S&H)

[ ] Send *English Standard Bible (ESV) Deficiencies* by several authors ($7.00 + $4.00 S&H)

[ ] Send *Strong's Micro-Print Concordance* by the Sherbornes ($21.00 + $8.00 S&H)

Books by D. A. Waite, Jr.

[ ] Send *The Doctored New Testament* by D. A. Waite, Jr. ($25+$5 S&H) Greek MSS differences shown, hardback

[ ] Send *Readability of A.V. (KJB)* by D. A. Waite, Jr. ($6+$3)

[ ] Send *4,114 Definitions from the Defined King James Bible* by D. A. Waite, Jr. ($7.00+$4.00 S&H)

Question And Answer Books by Dr. D. A. Waite

[ ] Send *The First 200 Questions Answered* by Dr. D. A. Waite ($15.00 + $7.00 S&H)

[ ] Send *The Second 200 Questions Answered* by Dr. D. A. Waite ($15.00 + $7.00 S&H)

[ ] Send *The Third 200 Questions Answered* by Dr. D. A. Waite ($15.00 + $7.00 S&H)

[ ] Send *The Fourth 200 Questions Answered* by Dr. D. A. Waite ($15.00 + $7.00 S&H)

[ ] Send *The Fifth 200 Questions Answered* by Dr. D. A. Waite ($15.00 + $7.00 S&H)

[ ] Send *The Sixth 200 Questions Answered* by Dr. D. A. Waite ($15.00 + $7.00 S&H)

[ ] Send *The Seventh 200 Questions Answered* by Dr. D. A. Waite ($15.00 + $7.00 S&H)

Send or Call Orders to:

THE BIBLE FOR TODAY

900 Park Ave., Collingswood, NJ 08108

Phone: 856-854-4452; FAX:--2464; Orders: 1-800 JOHN 10:9

E-Mail Orders: BFT@BibleForToday.org; Credit Cards OK

Pastor D. A. Waite, Th.D., Ph.D.

The 7ᵗʰ 200 Questions Answered

- **The Reason For This Book.** I have put into print six previous *200 Questions Answers books*. This present *200 Questions And Answers* book is the 7ᵗʰ in this important series. Though many have answered some of these questions before, these are my thoughtful answers based on the Bible and truth.

- **The Goal of This Book.** The goal has been to give to the readers some explanation of what our Bible For Today ministry believes on a number of important topics. Many of our friends do not know what we believe and where we stand on a number of questions. This book will inform them fully about these matters..

- **The Name of This Book.** By the title of the book, "*The Seventh 200 Questions Answered by Dr. D. A. Waite,*" it shows that this is the 7ᵗʰ book giving my answers to the many questions that have been asked me through the many years.

- **The Usefulness of This Book.** As you can see, unlike many books, this book has an elaborate thirteen-page "*Index of Words and Phrases*" in the back pages so the reader can look up any word or subject they wish to look into. With this Index, they can find it without difficulty. Some of the entries might seem trivial and unnecessary, but that depends on what is being searched. It is hoped that this Index will make this book a more useful tool than without it. It is also hoped that these will give you answers to questions you might have.

www.BibleForToday.org

BFT 4151   **ISBN #1-56848-110-4**

www.ingramcontent.com/pod-product-compliance
Lightning Source LLC
Chambersburg PA
CBHW071437090426
42737CB00011B/1695